State of Play

A Theatre Magazine

State of Play

Issue 1: Playwrights on Playwriting

Edited by DAVID EDGAR

Contributors: David Edgar, Peter Ansorge, Mark Ravenhill, Kevin Elyot, William Gaminara, Clare McIntyre, Winsome Pinnock, Rebecca Prichard, Andy de la Tour, Cheryl Martin, David Greig, Diane Samuels, Timberlake Wertenbaker, April de Angelis, Christopher Hampton, Peter Whelan, Sebastian Barry, John Mortimer, Bill Morrison, Anne Devlin, Conor McPherson, Nicholas Wright, Mike Bradwell, David Eldridge, Dusty Hughes, Phyllis Nagy

faber and faber

First published in 1999
by Faber and Faber Limited
3 Queen Square London WC1N 3AU

Photoset by Wilmaset Ltd, Wirral
Printed in England by Clays Ltd, St Ives plc

Sebastian Barry's contribution was first published as an introduction to *The Steward of Christendom* (Methuen Drama, 1997). Some of the material in Part One first appeared, in different form, in the *Sunday Times*, the *Guardian*, the *Times Literary Supplement* and the *Journal* of the Royal Society for the Encouragement of Arts, Manufactures and Commerce.

A CIP record for this book
is available from the British Library
ISBN 0-571-20096-6

2 4 6 8 10 9 7 5 3 1

Contents

Preface

This book marks the tenth year of two connected institutions. Founded in 1989, the University of Birmingham's MA in playwriting studies arose out of a self-help movement among British playwrights which itself emerged from the Theatre Writers' Union in the challenging years of the 1980s.

As part of a necessary reassertion of the importance of playwriting within the ecology of the British theatre, it was decided that the MA course would host an annual conference, on a different topic each year, to bring together playwrights, directors, actors, agents, academics, critics, publishers and playgoers to debate the most important current issues in the British theatre.

So although playwrights have always participated, the subject matter of the Birmingham Theatre Conference has ranged much wider than the state of new work. The first conference was on regional theatre ('Regional Accents') and began with a keynote lecture by the French playwright Michel Vinaver. In subsequent years the conference discussed the challenge to text-based performance ('Beyond Words'), theatre and nationhood ('National Stages'), the crisis of content ('All Passion Spent?'), musical theatre ('Facing the Music'), fact-based drama ('Reality Time'), and the heritage of thirty years of political theatre ('Better Red'). Running through all of them has been a series of passionate and occasionally fierce debates: between the text-based and the devised, opera and musicals, the popular against the élitist and the imaginative against the polemical.

But perhaps the most crucial conferences were two which did foreground the state of new writing. In 1991 'State of Play' set out to anatomize what seemed to be an exponential decline in the amount, quality and performance of new work in the British theatre; while seven years later 'About Now' celebrated a whole new generation of young writers who had emerged – despite all these predictions – in the intervening years.

Accordingly, the central section of this book consists largely (but not exclusively) of edited contributions to 'About Now', beginning with a television producer's provocative challenge to the very idea of a new golden age in the theatre, and ending with two very different views of the current state of play in stage and screen writing. In between, panellists discuss the reputed upsurge in plays by and about young men, the continued vibrancy of plays by women (including plays set in the past), the unique contribution of Irish playwrights to contemporary drama in Britain, the alleged decline in political theatre and the undeniable growth in theatrical autobiography.

Either side of this section are two newly written contributions. Drawing on the proceedings of all nine conferences, the introductory chapter seeks to place the current situation and prospects of British theatre within the context of the post-war era as a whole. In conclusion, the playwright Phyllis Nagy develops her argument (originally presented in one of the most passionate contributions to 'About Now') against what she sees as a narcissistic literalism in much contemporary new work of the 1990s, and in favour of a renewal of metaphor in the theatre.

Both the Birmingham course and its conference are based on the assumption that it is legitimate and even helpful for playwrights to come together to discuss their profession and the industries of which it is a part. Assembling this book has relied on the insights and the labour of the contributors; but it would not exist without the 214 speakers and panellists who have contributed to the Birmingham Theatre Conference (their names are listed at the back of the book); to the upwards of a thousand people who have attended it (many of them regularly), and particularly to the 115 playwriting students (many of whom are now contributing significantly to the story) for whom it was originally conceived. The conference has been enriched by the participation of collaborators, including Granada Television and Red Ladder Theatre Company (who co-hosted 'Reality Time' and 'Better Red' respectively), the director John Caird (who co-produced 'Facing the Music') and the Arts and Leisure Department of the City of Birmingham, which has contributed to and collaborated with the conference in a variety of ways over the years. The conference would not be celebrating its tenth birthday – or indeed any birthday at all – without a host of student helpers, the print designer (and bookseller) Duncan Fielden and most of all the administrator Amanda Cadman.

David Edgar, June 1990

PART ONE

Provocative Acts: British Playwriting in the Post-war Era and Beyond

David Edgar

Alone among the arts, the live theatre is in the present tense or it is nowhere. It is perhaps an index of the state of threat in which the British theatre currently finds itself that so much is being written about its past and speculated about its future. What is the same and what is different about now and then will determine whether there is a present to talk about in the next century.

Statistically, the 1990s began with cheer and ended with gloom. Between 1991 and 1998, seat prices in the English theatre rose by 50 per cent while attendances fell by 30 per cent. In terms of new theatre writing, the trajectory was the reverse, as the National's new plays continued to move as if on a conveyor belt from the Cottesloe via the Lyttelton into the West End, the Royal Court had its biggest ever box office advance with Conor McPherson's *The Weir*, and new work in the repertory sector found itself outperforming Shakespeare.

A new play boom amid a general gloom: if nothing else, this paradox exposes the big lie that new plays inevitably empty the building. Now and for the foreseeable future, the health of the British theatre is and will be inextricably bound up with the health of new writing.

It has not always been so, but it has been so for most of the post-war era. To understand the challenges, opportunities and dangers that we face in the new millennium, it is necessary to understand not only what has happened over the last ten years, but in the decades preceding, both in the theatre and in the culture as a whole. Having explored how cultural policy reflected wider political debates, up to and including Labour's 1997 election victory, it might be possible to speculate about where we all go from here.

Wave upon wave: new theatre writing 1956–1990

Previewed as a White Paper, and based on a Green Paper, the Arts Council's long-delayed 1996 report on drama in England in fact turned out to be red. In it, the Council stated as a basic principle that 'all drama should be contemporary, whether it is new, recently created, or established work from the classical repertoire that speaks to audiences of today'.

By using 'contemporary' to mean 'lively' or 'immediate', the document denied the existence of a category of drama written, performed and set now. This is a pity, because since the opening of *Look Back in Anger* on 8 May 1956 at the Royal Court, it has been generally if intermittently accepted that contemporary work in this sense has been central to the project of the British theatre. It has not been ever thus. Indeed, there have really only been three periods when British drama was dominated by new writing, none of them lasting much more than a quarter of a century. The glories of the Elizabethan–Jacobean period – Shakespeare and his contemporaries and successors – fall between around 1590 and 1620; the so-called Restoration period begins in the late 1670s and effectively ends with the death of George Farquhar in 1707; and the period between 1890 and 1914 gives us the whole of Wilde, the best of Granville-Barker, Pinero, Barrie and Galsworthy, and Bernard Shaw from *Widowers' Houses* via *Man and Superman* to *Pygmalion*. Between them there were periods of huge dramatic achievement, but not of great writing. Almost all the great British actors (from Garrick and Macready via Irving to the heyday of Olivier and Gielgud) are at their zenith in periods of writerly dearth; as are many of the great achievements of production and design.

Further, all of the previous golden ages seem to have had two defining characteristics: they occurred in the wake of great national upheavals; and there was a new audience hungry to come to terms with the consequent social and cultural change. All of the great periods of British theatre writing have been in the aftermath of great national triumphs, at the point where the loss of the old calls into question the rise of the new. Shakespeare, twenty years after the Armada, interrogates the new Renaissance man, freeing himself from the bonds of feudalism. A decade or so after the defeat of the Puritan commonwealth, Wycherley and Etherege challenge as well as celebrate the amoral atmosphere and ethos of Restoration London. And the challenge to triumphant industrial capitalism posed by Shaw, Barker and in his way Wilde comes twenty or thirty years after the peak of Britain's great industrial and imperial achievements; as these playwrights too bit deeply into the souring fruits of victory.

4

The epoch of British theatre that began in 1956 also addressed the consequences of upheaval in conversation with an audience whose lives were changed by it. The upheaval in question was of course the Second World War, and the vast social changes that flowed therefrom; not least the welfare state and the 1944 Education Act, which allowed a whole new generation of young men (in particular) to reach levels of educational achievement their parents could not have dreamt of.

The first wave of 1956 playwrights, from John Osborne, Arnold Wesker and John Arden to the early Edward Bond, confronted the consequences of this working-class empowerment, in some cases with enthusiasm, in some cases with alarm. For the generation that followed, forged in the youth revolt of the late 1960s, the questions were much more aggressively political. They were about the limits of social democracy and the welfare state (in the jargon of the time, the debate between liberal reform and socialist revolution). While in the early 1980s the ground shifted once more, as women, black and gay playwrights confronted the questions of difference and identity which had emerged in the 1960s and 1970s.

True, there were major writers who stand outside this trajectory, or whose work relates to it only peripherally (as Sheridan and Goldsmith emerge out of nothing towards the end of the eighteenth century). The writers whose early work arose out of absurdism, Harold Pinter and Tom Stoppard, are exceptional in every sense (not least by way of turning to political drama in middle age). There is a rich tradition of serious writers for the commercial mainstream (Michael Frayn, Peter Nichols, Simon Gray, Alan Bennett) who relate to the model only tangentially. But from 1956 certainly until the late 1980s there have been wave upon wave of playwrights self-consciously addressing the social, political and cultural state of the nation in conversation with each other, and with those who followed and preceded them.

As is the way with generational change, each new wave sought to overthrow what had gone before. For the Royal Court writers of the late 1950s, the enemy was clear. History is now a great deal kinder to Terence Rattigan, then perceived as the embodiment of the smug self-satisfaction of the theatre of the early 1950s. But there is no doubt that the theatre of that time reflected a general urge in British society to withdraw from the upheavals of the 1940s, to reach back, as Peter Brook puts it, 'towards a memory of lost grace'. The generic early

1950s set was that of the drawing room or indeed the country house, the generic form the light social comedy or the whodunnit. The big hits of 1955 were the musicals *Salad Days*, a preposterously anodyne picture of undergraduate arcadia, and *The Boyfriend*, an ersatz recreation of 1920s flapperland.

The Angry Young Men who emerged in the novel and the theatre thus had at least one obvious enemy. There were, however, two others. One was the culture from which most of them had escaped: John Osborne bitterly resented the narrow, lower-middle-class culture he'd left behind. Another was the mass popular culture beginning to be imported from America.

So although Osborne, Wesker and their contemporaries famously moved their plays out of the drawing room into the kitchen (although there isn't a sink in *Look Back in Anger*, there is a ironing board), neither they nor their heroes were entirely happy with the move. Osborne's Jimmy Porter is hostile to the aristocratic, country-house England of his wife's family, but also (and perhaps more vehemently) to the working-class yobs who threaten his Sunday night at the cinema. While in Wesker's *Roots*, Beattie Bryant's great epiphany at the end of the play – in which she finds her own voice and speaks in it for herself and her class – is not a celebration of 'the slop singers and the pop writers and the film makers and women's magazines', but very precisely a rejection of the 'whole stinkin' commercial world' in favour of bringing a higher culture to the masses. And this debate reaches its climax in 1966 with Edward Bond's *Saved*, in which a group of young working-class men stone a baby to death on stage (a play which Bond described famously as 'almost irresponsibly optimistic').

For these writers, then, the key question was simple: what would be the ultimate effect on British culture of the democratization that had taken both the writers and their audiences out of the working and lower-middle classes and into the new intelligentsia? For my generation, the one that followed, such writers were irredeemably compromised by the culture that they purported to challenge but seemed eager to embrace. Certainly we didn't see the function of high art as civilizing the masses, rather the other way round. And we were enabled by three new factors to take a much more radical view of the theatre experience. The first was the abolition of stage censorship in August 1968, which enabled work of an overtly sexual (and political) character, but which also allowed work that was topical or indeed improvised. The second factor was the great expansion of state subsidy to small-scale theatre in the late 1960s, which enabled the third factor, the explosion of alternative theatre spaces and forms variously dubbed the underground, the alternative and the fringe. Perhaps the defining characteristic of our generation, at least at the beginning, was that it sought a new audience outside theatre buildings – indeed, sometimes out of buildings altogether – often in collaboration with an alternative, non-literary avant-garde theatre form then called performance art, in collective advocacy and celebration of the revolutionary spirit of the age. And I believe that much that was good about British theatre in the years that followed – its boldness, its imagination, its commitment, its collective methods, its populism and accessibility – was present in that heady time.

However, as the 1970s developed, this fragile unity between political theatre and performance art, between the verbal and the visual, the university and the art college, the theatre of thought and the theatre of imagination, began to splinter, as (first of all) the performance artists split off from political theatre makers to form their own performance circuits with their own devotees. Then there was the division within the political theatre movement, as some theatre makers continued to seek a working-class audience outside theatre buildings, whilst others sought to make a career in the mainstream theatre, moving away from the streets and on to the stages of the great institutional theatres in London: the Royal Court, the Royal Shakespeare Company and the National Theatre.

The political plays of the 1970s shared a number of characteristics, of which the most important were a hostility to domestic and familial settings, a determination to write plays set in present-day England (unlike, largely, Bond, Arden and Bertolt Brecht), and a shared model of what had made that England what it was. In essence, David Hare's *Plenty*, Howard Brenton's *The Churchill Play* and my *Destiny* pursued elements of a single grand narrative which very roughly went like this: Britain had been on the right side in the war against Hitler, but had squandered its moral capital afterwards. There'd been a chance after the war to create a genuine egalitarian, emancipatory socialism, but it was implemented too half-heartedly by the 1945–51 Labour government and the opportunity was lost. The country then held a kind of party in the 1950s and 1960s, squandering its post-imperial riches, and in the 1970s had gone into free-fall political, economic and moral decline, at the end of which, it was assumed, final collapse would occur and 'true socialism' would emerge phoenix-like from the ashes.

And, of course, something new did indeed emerge in British political life at the end of the 1970s, but it bore little relationship to true socialism. More profound than our embarrassment, however, was a sense which had been growing through the later 1970s that the emergent social issues were not to be constrained within the iron determinism of class politics, but were to be found within the crevices of the much more fragile, porous but intriguing geology of difference. So the third wave of new playwrights – those who emerged in the early to mid 1980s – didn't answer to names like David, John and Howard but to names like Sarah, Bryony, Louise and Clare. In 1979 there were two currently-writing, nationally-known women playwrights in Britain (Pam Gems and Caryl Churchill). Ten years later there were two dozen, whose work had dominated the decade. Typically, the Royal Court was in the forefront of this sea change: between 1956 and 1980 eight per cent of the plays presented at the Court were by women; in the 1980s it was 38 per cent. As its then artistic director Max Stafford-Clark told the 'State of Play' conference (1991): 'If we could find a play called *When I was a Girl I was Not Quite a Bent Catholic*, we would stage it immediately.'

The emergence of this major new force in British theatre writing was not as easy or uncontentious as this cheerful quotation might imply. As energetic and festive, but also as radical and even angrier than the counterculture of the late 1960s, the women's liberation movement and its theatre threw down a challenge not just to the institutional theatre and its repertoire but to the alternative theatre as well.

As Susan Todd put it at 'Regional Accents' (1990), the explosion of new women's theatre met a 'desperate need to speak the unspoken'; a need arising partly out of the limitations and aridities of the political theatre that went before. By placing the politics of the mother–daughter relationship at the centre of their art, Charlotte Keatley and Sharman Macdonald were among those who challenged the notion (implied in many of the socialist plays of the 1970s) that politics inevitably stop at the front door. Other writers – like Pam Gems and Timberlake Wertenbaker – took on male readings of history and myth: with Gems rewriting the biographies of Queen Christina and Edith Piaf, and Wertenbaker reassessing English history in *The Grace of Mary Traverse* and Greek myth in *The Love of the Night-*

ingale. And new women writers – from Keatley in Manchester via Macdonald, Liz Lochhead and Rona Munro in Scotland to Anne Devlin and Christina Reid in Northern Ireland – were a central part of a self-conscious reassertion of a theatre of the regions and nations of the United Kingdom which was another underestimated feature of the decade. While at the same time, other communities of difference were engaging in not always polite (and certainly not one-way) debate with their audiences: as gay, lesbian and sometimes black and Asian writers sought to articulate and define their identities in often uncomfortable relation to each other. The complexities of the relationship between gender, sexual orientation, class and nation was most succinctly put by Liz Lochhead at 'National Stages' (1993) when she affirmed: 'I think my country is women.'

On this reading, one could see post-'56 British theatre as a kind of three-act drama, reflecting the political debates which surrounded it. So, Act One asked how the working class would use its new-found wealth and power; Act Two proposed a drastic answer to that question; and Act Three articulated a radical politics based not on class but on race, gender and sexuality. But while each sought to confront and overthrow what had preceded it, a particular dialectic slithered through all of them.

At the climax of David Hare's 1994 National Theatre play *The Absence of War*, the leader of the Labour Party breaks with his written text and opens his heart to his audience. At last, one thinks, he will express his own convictions, uncompromised by political calculation. After a page of passion, however, he becomes aware of the dangers of honesty, and returns, stuttering slightly, to the words of the speech prepared for him.

Such failures of nerve pepper the work of the social dramatists of the last forty-five years, back to and including *Look Back in Anger*. Most people remember the 'no good brave causes left' speech, the *cri de coeur* which Jimmy Porter delivers to his friend Cliff, but not that it ends bathetically, with Cliff being handed not a revolutionary placard or manifesto but a clean shirt. There is, however, another oft-repeated moment, almost precisely opposite in meaning, in which a person – most usually a woman – finds their own articulacy and successfully expresses it. At the end of Arnold Wesker's *Roots*, the working-class Beattie Bryant has to confront the fact that her communist boyfriend has let her down and is not coming to visit her and her family in their

Norfolk home, and that she must rely on her own language rather than his, and finds her articulacy thereby. Her epiphany is directly echoed in Trevor Griffiths' *Comedians*, Willy Russell's *Educating Rita* and Jim Cartwright's *Road*.

These two devices express the contest that dominates post-war British drama. The descent from bang into whimper dramatizes the failure of honest conviction to defeat the cynical sham of post-war life. The hitherto silent finding voice expresses a belief in their emancipation from social and political constraints. The debate between those two poles – jaded failure versus youthful optimism, deflated rhetoric versus achieved articulacy – runs through from John Osborne certainly to Charlotte Keatley.

But what both poles shared was an assumption that the basic fault line continued to be between a belief in cultural and political emancipation on the one hand, and a descent into disillusioned and cynical traditionalism on the other. Increasingly, however, political and cultural conservatism re-emerged not as a last refuge but a first port of call, and it was clear that emancipation had been dumped in the same skip as letting it all hang out and doing it in the road. For all the energy and vigour of the theatre of difference in the 1980s, the peak appeared to have passed by the end of the decade, and the theatre of difference and identity had joined the Angry Young Man and the Revolutionary Playwrights of the 1970s among things that had been.

The new spirit that had entered and sought to dominate the theatre was no longer that of political emancipation but economic liberalism. Between 1956 and the early 1980s the theatre had been transformed by the end of empire, the student uprising of the late 1960s and the women's liberation movement, as had the culture as a whole. The changes brought about in the Thatcher period were as profound as any which preceded it.

Cultural geometry

If one had to sum up the change that the post-war period brought about in the left view of the world, it would be the move from a binary to a triangular model of political (and indeed cultural) life. Traditionally, the left saw the world as a confrontation between two poles, the bourgeoisie and the working class. Since the late 1970s it has been increasingly hard to evade the idea of politics as a conversation between corners of a triangle: top-down state socialism (the command economies of the east, the state-led social democracies that were developed during and after the war in the west); the revived free-market liberalism of Margaret Thatcher and Ronald Reagan; and something else (much less clear) which posed a challenge to both – variously dubbed grassroots activism, participatory democracy, new social forces, rainbow coalitions and, indeed, various 'third ways'.

This geometry is reflected in the cultural industries. The old debate between high art and popular entertainment has been replaced with a three-way conversation between three distinct models of what and who art is for, and how best to bring those aims about.

First, there is the patrician model, which sees art's role as ennobling, its realm the nation, its organisational form the institution, its repertoire the established canon and works aspiring to join it, its base audience the cultural élite. In traditional opposition to the patrician model is that of the popular: seeing art's primary purpose as entertainment, its realm the market-place, its form the business, its audience mass. In contrast to both is the provocative (both in content and form): defining the role of the arts as challenging, its realm the community, its form the collective, its audience diverse but united in its commitment to change.

The story of the post-war arts – in Britain and indeed Europe – can be seen as a conversation between at least two of these models; and at its best a debate between all three.

For the twenty-five years following the war, the cultural policies of most European nations were aimed at widening the audience for the traditional high arts. As Robert Hewison argues in *Culture and Consensus*, this strategy informed the Reithian BBC and defined the ethos of Britain's Arts Council from its foundation by John Maynard Keynes to its high point during Jennie Lee's tenure as Arts Minister (1964–70) and under the chairmanship of Lord Goodman (1965–72). Often in conscious opposition to mass popular culture, though frequently in alliance with the high avant-garde, this first phase was sustained by a generally accepted idea of the division between high and low culture and a preference for the former. At its narrowest and smoothest, it was to be heard on the Third Programme; provoked by dispossession, it emerged as the outcry of both Jimmy Porter and Beattie Bryant against the poverty of mass popular culture. If its mission statement was Matthew Arnold's classic statement of the patrician principle of criticism (that 'disinterested endeavour to learn and propagate the best that is known and thought in the world') then its slogan was Keynes's ringing declaration: 'Death to Hollywood.'

But then, in the 1960s and 1970s, this approach came under challenge from the new cultural left that had been enabled and inspired by the success of the provocative in the political sphere. As the activists of 1968 moved from the streets into city government (from the anarcho-collectivist Movimento in Rome and Bologna to our own GLC), they brought with them a hostility to high art and a rejection of the patrician principles of extending its reach. Instead, they sought to encourage autonomous activity by the grassroots (sometimes for festive, more often with subversive purposes in mind). Indeed, the generic art form of the short-lived provocative hegemony in the great cities of Europe was the carnival: a synthesis of the visually orientated avant-garde and radical populism that reached its theatrical apogee in American companies like the Bread and Puppet Theatre and the Living Theatre, and in Europe with the alliance between communist popular festivals and the work of Dario Fo.

What happened next – and 'next' is of course the Thatcher period – is not as simple as it looks. To see Conservative arts policy as merely monetarism plus philistinism is to underestimate the importance of cultural policy to the project as a whole. Thatcherism was essentially a counter-revolutionary movement against the perceived collapse of traditional values (including cultural values) in the late 1960s and 1970s, itself the result of two complementary movements of the post-war world. First was the clutch of reforms associated with the 1940s: the New Deal in America, social democracy in Europe, the welfare state in Britain. These reforms aspired to counter the anarchy of the market-place – the perceived cause of slump and war – by removing some of industry from the market-place (nationalization) and some of the risks from life (welfare state); the result would be to create situations of social solidarity and coherence which would prevent western Europe going down either the right or left wing revolutionary road.

In retrospect, however, Thatcherites perceived the welfare state as removing the disciplines of the market-place: if your industries were nationalized they didn't have to make a profit, if you had a welfare state you didn't have to work. If the state knew best, then there was a real danger that society would be infantilized. This thesis was confirmed by the 1960s and the revolt of large sections of society against its constrictions, most notably, it was observed, a revolt by people working in nationalized industries – striking miners, railwaymen, dockers – and those benefiting from the welfare state, especially students (and indeed their teachers) in higher education. Far from providing evidence of social cohesion and solidarity, these groups in particular were seen as losing all self control and indulging in a riot of demand. As the 1960s turned into the 1970s and the protesting students were joined first by striking workers and then by sections of the urban poor in challenging the limits of the post-war consensus, so Thatcher's intellectuals decided that the way to counter these developments was not by legislation or command (as both Edward Heath and Richard Nixon had tried and failed to do) but by reimposing the disciplines of the market and removing the conditions under which revolt could flourish. Thus the way to stop workers striking was to privatize their industries, and the way to make the unemployed, students and indeed teachers and lecturers stop whingeing was to threaten their incomes.

So at the very heart of the Thatcherite reading of the post-war era there was a fundamental duality: the conformist, statist, authoritarian 1940s were seen as enabling the nonconformist, hyper-individualistic, anarchist 1960s and 1970s. And as a consequence the counter-attack was dualistic too: in its attack on the 1940s it was libertarian, promising to free the people from the shackles of state control, Big Brother and what was dubbed the 'nanny state'. On the other hand, against the 1960s it was authoritarian, seeking to reimpose traditional family values and disciplines. And that circle was squared by the argument that over-mighty government was responsible for anarchy, by removing people's sense of responsibility for the consequences of their own actions.

In the cultural sector, a form of the same model applied. In the 1940s, it was argued, state subsidy was introduced to protect high art from the vicissitudes of the market, so that it could make its contribution to the cohesive mission of the welfare state (again, on the assumption that the beneficent state knew best what high art was and why it was good for people). However, in the same way that the removal of market disciplines from industry promoted indulgence, so in the 1960s art became oppositional for its own sake, challenging the very values of civilization it was supposed to promote. And as the beneficiaries of the welfare state had turned against their benefactors, so artists used their Arts Council grants to attack the very idea of high art, and to promote ideas that were seen as subversive if not revolutionary. In short, the hegemony of the airily patrician had enabled the subversively provocative to seize control. The counter-revolutionary strategy was to use the market as a wedge to detach the provocative from the patrician in order to destroy it.

Thus in Thatcherism's laboratory period, as it prepared its policies in the late 1970s, the market was seen as the sole motor of arts development, for ostensibly libertarian reasons. Less than a fortnight after her 1979 election victory, Mrs Thatcher's first arts minister, Norman St John Stevas, asserted that private funding not only provided 'an alternative source of finance', but also had the merit of 'avoiding or neutralizing some of the dangers of state patronage, such as censorship and conformity and the promotion of what I might venture to call "establishment art"'.

However, this anti-authoritarian, 'let a hundred flowers bloom' view of arts privatization was countered by a much more traditional and conservative perspective, in which the market was not so much a liberator as a policeman. Shortly after the 1987 general election, Stevas's successor Richard Luce made a famous attack on those in the arts world 'who have yet to be weaned away from the welfare state mentality – the attitude that the taxpayer owes them a living', going on to insist that 'the only real test of our ability to succeed is whether or not we can attract enough customers.' Similarly, Douglas Mason of the Thatcherite think-tank the Adam Smith Institute criticized subsidy not for stifling initiative and invention but rather for encouraging 'élitism' and 'self-indulgence'.

By the mid 1980s, then, the strategy was clear. The 1940s high-art-as-civilizer model had enabled the 1960s art-as-subverter model to grow and flourish. The way to return to the traditional, socially cohesive nature of the arts was, paradoxically, to commercialize them. Under the discipline of the market-place, the producers of art would be forced to provide what its consumers wanted, which was that which would be least likely to disrupt and disturb. This use of liberal economic means to achieve conservative cultural and political objectives was the great political invention of the Thatcher era. As the lady herself put it, 'Economics are the method; the object is to change the heart and soul of the nation' (*Sunday Times*, 3 May 1981). No wonder that this principle was applied not only to municipal housing and the provision of medical services but also to the arts.

Hence the great cultural paradox of the 1980s: while the commercial was aestheticized (in every area of life, from interior decoration via advertising, fashion and graphic design to food), the arts themselves were commercialized. Hence, too, the creation by the popular market of a real cultural invention. Mrs Thatcher's first speech as party leader criticized 'the deliberate attack on our heritage and our great past.' Popular in form, patrician in content, the heritage industry *is* cultural Thatcherism. Of course it had an economic dimension; as the Arts Council itself put it, 'the arts are to British tourism what the sun is to Spain'. More specifically, the then secretary of state Virginia Bottomley said in May 1996, the British film industry should act as a standard bearer to 'promote our country, our cultural heritage and our tourist trade', going on to cite the recent explosion in reverent Jane Austen adaptations, and remarking, 'If we have got the country houses and the landscapes, they should be shown off on film, particularly as we approach the millennium.' But it goes beyond tourism into cultural politics: Bottomley's statement was made in a week when the chairman of the Arts Council vetoed an award to a film exploring the homosexuality of the painter Francis Bacon. Let a hundred flowers bloom, but only if they are embedded in an English country garden.

Indeed, the contribution of film and television drama to the heritage industry is a clear example of the way in which libertarian economic means lead on to conservative cultural ends. The performing arts and broadcasting were the last great institutions to be sent to market, long after the universities, medicine and the law; the great reform of British television took place under John Major, and imitative reforms in the live performing arts are still in contest. But as with NHS and education reform, the starting point has been the extension of the myth of the universal customer – the notion that there is no essential difference in my dealings with my bank, my newsagent, my grocer, my electricity supplier, my doctor, my football team or my child's school – into parts hitherto unreached.

The model for this is of course the BBC, which faced up to a precipitous real-terms decline in licence-fee income in the 1980s and early 1990s not by a stated policy of going downmarket, but by restructuring. This consisted of the separation of the BBC's commissioning and programming from production, so that its in-house producers now compete with independents, on supposedly equal terms, to sell programmes to BBC Broadcast which schedules them, promotes them and puts them out. One stated intention of this move was to reduce costs; but a more fundamental aim was to shift power from the setter-uppers to the putter-outers, and thus to tame the creative pretensions of supposedly élitist producers on the public's behalf. In practice, this removes responsibility for television's relationship with its audience from those who should properly be concerned to develop it as a two-way conversation, handing it over to the retrospective – and thus inevitably conservative – calculations of market research (hence, of course, the explosion of cops, docs and classic serials). Exacerbated by the palpable reduction of the institutional cure of the dramatic forms and the people who work in them (there is now no one who puts out programmes with overall responsibility for radio drama), the New BBC is the clearest possible demonstration of how restructuring for the market creates conservative programming. You don't actually have to issue management diktats. You don't need to.

Essentially consisting of a shift of power from the producer to the consumer, these developments reflect more general trends. In *The Age of Extremes*, historian Eric Hobsbawm argues that the principal event of the post-war era in the arts has been the death of the avant-garde, as a result of the emergence of a mass, market-led popular culture that forced the traditional high arts into a ghetto and squeezed the avant-garde out altogether. Hobsbawm also notes the way in which this move was, if not caused, then at least aided and abetted by a strange alliance between commerce and fashionable literary and philosophical theory.

It is easy to recognize this model in Britain. If the early years of the post-war era saw a patrician attempt to reverse the tide of transatlantic populism and the 1960s a provocative attack on the patrician on all fronts, then the 1980s saw an assault by commercialism on the patrician values of the great institutions which by 1990 had virtually eliminated the provocative, as it was intended to do. Thus, in music the essential contest was between the traditional orchestras and lyric companies and the populist challenge of Earls Court opera and the Three Tenors; in television between the Reithian tradition and the Birtist challenge; in theatre between the patrician values of the national companies and the no-nonsense populism of a reinvigorated West End. Sure, each medium had its provocative wing: but who would argue that the musical avant-garde, feminist theatre or even Channel 4 were as strong or as clear in their challenge to the patrician and the popular as they had been in the mid 1980s? Indeed, for all its initial radicalism, one could see Channel 4's diversity as a paradigm for an increasingly pluralistic production system at the BBC. The channel may have set out to provide an alternative to the homogenous mass populism of industrial television; what it actually did was provide a model for a commercialized BBC.

Between the mid 1950s and the mid 1980s, the provocative taught the patrician a language with which to defend itself against the populist; by the mid 1990s, everyone was talking like marketing managers. In so far as there was music, television or stage drama directed at those outside the mainstream, it was on the strict under-standing that we are all niches now. It is not that the provocative ever sought to take over (how could it and remain itself?), but rather that without a provocative agenda somewhere in the vocabulary, the patrician biodegrades into the conventional (the concentration on a narrowing range of popular classics in both theatre and television), and the popular into the plebeian and the philistine.

There is one final irony in all of this. As Hobsbawm points out, the great paradox of the last decades is the way in which the anti-high-art practice of the late 1960s counter-culture was theoreticized in the 1970s by a progressive intellectual challenge to the high versus popular art distinction, celebrating hitherto disregarded forms and genres like the television soap opera, and thus giving academic respectability, in the 1980s, to letting the market rip. Similarly, by rejecting the distinction between high and popular art, the municipal anarcho-populists of the 1970s opened cultural policy out into the hitherto ignored (if not despised) 'commercial' realms of electronic music, broadcasting and fashion; which in its turn appeared to justify those politicians of the 1980s more sympathetic to the commercial in rushing pell-mell into the market-place.

Thus, in municipal strategy as in post-modern theory, a supposedly provocative challenge to the patrician served only to give a progressive imprimatur to populism. It is an exaggeration to say that the counter-culture set out to replace *Hamlet*, Keats and Beethoven with Dario Fo, Bob Dylan and Velvet Underground but ended up giving a progressive imprimatur to *Casualty*, Jeffrey Archer and the Spice Girls. But it's not *too* far from the truth.

Death of the new: theatre 1988–92

The full extent of what had happened to the theatre during all of this was only clear at the end of the 1980s, and the gloomy consequences were the main subject matter of the early conferences in Birmingham. Like broadcasting, theatre is a mixed economy, and in both cases the advance guard of change was linguistic, as an increasingly beleaguered funding system offered a whole series of supposedly foolproof commercial strategies to theatres on a sale or go-under basis: from subscription to sponsorship, from improved catering to zappy marketing to board restructuring. Underpinning all of these supposed panaceas was the idea that directors couldn't run theatres, and that a new class of 'executive producers' with exponentially extended staffs could bring the mysterious magic of good business practice to bear on the undoubted difficulties of companies trying to run theatres designed in and for the optimistic 1960s rather than the altogether grimmer world of the 1980s and 1990s.

Thus, under pressure from the Arts Council, theatres up and down the land drew up mission statements, repositioned their corporate image (this meant redesigning the letterhead) and set out to attract corporate sponsorship to pay for it: the renamed 'Royal' National Theatre offered sponsoring firms 'increased corporate awareness' and 'prestigious entertainment facilities'; the already Royal Shakespeare Company assured businessmen that it could 'tailor a project to suit a company's individuality and offer a high return on a sponsorship investment'.

Eventually, all of this presentation began to affect what was presented. It was not just a matter of commercial companies withdrawing sponsorship from plays they saw as difficult or offensive, though this happened. Gradually, too, the theatre changed its attitude to its audience. Instead of addressing 'playgoers', who might expect the experience of playgoing to be challenging as well as confirming, actors were serving 'customers', who as we know are always right. As a consequence, by the end of the 1980s it was often hard to tell rep programmes apart. There was, for a kick-off, a nationwide epidemic of adaptations (up from 6 per cent of the repertoire in the 1970s to 20 per cent in the late 1980s), suggesting that theatre had lost confidence in itself and was turning to other media for validation. Then it became harder and harder to see original plays you didn't know by heart. In

1988, if you went to the theatre in England and didn't see *The Tempest* or *Gaslight* they gave you a small cash prize. In the years following, there were major outbreaks of *Seagull*s, *Blithe Spirit*s, *Doll's House*s and various Ostrovskis; as the 1990s draw to an end, it appears that it is once again *Three Sisters*es and *Hamlet*s that are breeding beyond epidemiological control.

The main victim of these developments was new work. As the then Arts Council drama director Ian Brown pointed out at 'State of Play', the late 1980s saw a precipitate decline in the amount of new work presented. From 1970 to 1985, new work formed roughly 12 per cent of the repertoire of the main houses of the regional and London repertory theatres. From 1985 to 1990 it dropped to 7 per cent. Whether as a consequence or a cause, the box office *performance* of new work declined as well; in the early 1980s new plays were doing as well as, if not sometimes better than, the rest of straight drama; by the late 1980s a significant gap had grown. Some theatres, like the Royal Court in London, continued to present a repertoire dominated by new work; other companies, like the RSC, continued to do new plays as a matter of policy, but increasingly concentrated in small theatre spaces (at 'State of Play', Anthony Minghella was particularly critical of the deleterious effect of studio theatres in encouraging what he called 'mumble plays – triangles in rectangular rooms'). And all of this was justified by a growing belief, among directors in particular, that new work had run out of steam. Hardly a week passed without the *Guardian* and the *Independent* having some sort of stab at new theatre writing: if by writers under thirty, it was ill-formed and unfinished; if they were over thirty, it was jaded and tired. It became *de rigueur* for directors under (and even on occasions a little over) thirty to announce that they couldn't be bothered with the triviality of the contemporary, and they certainly couldn't cope with the trauma of having a living writer in the rehearsal room. Instead, they were either doing increasingly operatic and continental versions of not always unjustly neglected European classics on dangerously raked stages, or endless productions of the twenty or so sure-fire classical pops. That this is not an exclusively British phenomenon was revealed by Michel Vinaver, whose excoriating keynote address at 'Regional Accents' demonstrated how French funding policy had created a new sovereignty of directors who saw themselves as the primary creative figures and had created by default a new writing culture not of dialogue but of soliloquy.

Meanwhile, in the small scale, those companies still operating and still doing new plays were not engaging writers to write them. The challenge to conventional text-based theatre was the subject of the fourth Birmingham Theatre Conference. Held in the somewhat shell-shocked atmosphere of the weekend following Labour's defeat at the 1992 general election, 'Beyond Words' was essentially a contest between the advocates of the individually written theatre text (whose primacy was passionately defended by Arnold Wesker) and the collaborative ethos of live art. Thus, Hilary Westlake of Lumiere and Son questioned whether the writer of the spoken text was 'necessarily the same person as the person who comes up with the concept'; Denise Wong revealed that Black Mime Theatre Company 'didn't want to be bound by a writer'. Clearly, some companies devise for financial reasons: in the mid 1980s, as the Theatre Writers' Union discovered, eight out of nine of the new plays presented by funded small-scale companies in the West Midlands were either devised or written by a company member; while in Manchester a 1992 survey revealed that only a third of the companies which presented new plays had ever employed an outside writer. And this trend was of course supported by a growing intellectual challenge to the primacy of the individually written text – a challenge that could call upon the full force of contemporary literary theory in its support.

Overshadowing all of this in sheer scale was the renewed and indeed in some senses reinvented stage form that symbolized the 1980s most profoundly. It is now clear that, in box office terms, the through-composed hi-tech musical can claim not only to be the most successful new stage form of the 1980s, but perhaps the most successful of all time. There is no precedent for the longevity of so large a number of stage shows. Through the four corners of the globe the *Evita* and *Les Misérables* images are as familiar as the Amex logo and the McDonald's M. On 19 June 1997 *Cats* became the longest-running musical ever on Broadway; there is no reason for *Phantom of the Opera* ever to close.

That this phenomenon has not been greeted with universal good favour is something of an understatement. Speaking at the 1995 conference ('All Passion Spent?'), John Bull of Sheffield University condemned the musical as ideologically conservative and creatively reactionary, both paradigm and cause of a theatre of escapism and nostalgia (put starkly by Michael Billington: 'dance is the enemy of art'). This view was, however, countered by writer-director Neil Bartlett, who defended the musical as a form uniquely possessed by its audience; for him, the ideal show is one to which a member of the audience could happily escort his boyfriend *and* his mother.

For Bull and Bartlett, the musical theatre is the clearest battleground between a theatre which sets out to challenge and disturb a supine audience (as Howard Brenton put it, the theatre that prides itself in 'pissing in the audience's eyeballs'), and a theatre which is the collective possession of producer and consumer, in mutual pursuit of pleasure. In 'All Passion Spent?' this argument was between straight theatre and the musical; in 'Facing the Music' (1995) the cudgels were taken up by the directors and composers of contemporary opera, who criticized *Les Misérables* and *Saigon Rose* co-author Alain Boublil for a musical aesthetic that had hardly moved on from Verdi. To this, Boublil responded that before it became élitist, opera had been a place where people of all backgrounds had come together for an experience that was intended to please, and he was happy to proclaim his work as a continuation of that tradition. The two positions were put perhaps most simply by Bartlett and librettist Nick Dear. At 'Facing the Music' Dear asked: 'When did you hear a musical with surprising opinions?' At 'All Passion Spent', Bartlett inquired whether anyone in the room had ever embraced a lover with the words, 'Oh darling, they're playing our speech.'

Whether culturally benign or malign, the practical effects of the rise of the musical have been clear and dramatic. The big musicals have converted the playgoing experience from regular theatre attendance to the occasional slam-bang treat; by exposing major classical directors, designers and actors to the market, musicals have transformed the culture of the subsidized rehearsal rooms to which these artists returned. Whether for good or ill, the musical was the Trojan horse by which the consumer-orientated principles of the market were infiltrated into the subsidized theatre.

Not surprisingly, this has had, and will have, institutional conse-quences. Unlike straight theatre, the through-composed musical is made by small independent teams presenting ideas to commissioning producers, an institutional model much closer to Channel 4 than to the Royal Shakespeare Company. Throughout the 1980s the arts funding system promoted the idea that managers were better at running theatres than artists (that is, better than George Devine at the Court,

Peter Hall and Trevor Nunn at the RSC, Richard Eyre at the National and Jude Kelly at Leeds), with the consequence that theatres became obsessed with ticket yield rather than audience share and priced regular theatregoing out of the market. While in the 1990s the idea of the 'presenting' (as opposed to the producing or receiving) house allowed theatre managers to dream of following the health service and now the BBC in separating out in-house production in order to disempower it, slash its costs and eventually cut it off.

A decline in audiences, financial cutbacks, a crisis of confidence, rampant commercialism, a hostile culture, a haemorrhage in the production of new work: this was one view at least of the theatre world of the early 1990s. But while some of its aspects would be familiar today, there have been two major developments. One was the discovery that reports of the collapse of new theatre writing in Britain had been greatly exaggerated. The other was the realization that the difficulties of electing a Labour government had been overestimated as well.

New Model

As with the Conservatives, Labour's policies for culture mirror its overall strategy. Like the Conservatives, too, Labour's policies have changed between opposition and government. Labour came into office with a considerable arts agenda, developed through the Kinnock and into the Smith and Blair eras by Mark Fisher. The pre-1992 statement, *Arts and Media: our cultural future*, was strongly influenced by the cultural critic Ken Worpole and mounted a rigorous and coherent challenge to the high–popular art divide, with a tendency to favour the modern over the pre-electronic media (its solution to widening access to opera was not to tour it but to put it on video). Five years on, *Create the Future* had lost six pages and a certain amount of edge, while gaining an epigraph by Ruskin and a radial diagram of the cultural industries, with 'tools of the trade' on the outer circle, 'associated activities' and 'distribution and delivery' in the middle, and an inner ring of 'live performance' surrounding a creative core of composers, painters, designers, performers and writers. Beyond a continued celebration of the economic contribution of the cultural industries, its overall perspective was less clear.

Now that it is in power, the Blair government's attitude to the arts and culture does appear to be sharply distinguished from the tax-and-grant thrust of his predecessors. Proverbially, the prime minister is not interested in the arts that cost money, but only in the arts that make money. His culture secretary Chris Smith takes a more inclusive attitude. In the introduction to his 1998 book *Creative Britain*, Smith names his key themes as access, excellence, education and economic value, without, however, saying much about what happens when these admirable principles collide. Excellence – which can of course conflict with access and certainly with economic value – is defined as using government support 'to underpin the best, and the most innovative, and the things that would not otherwise find a voice', which are of course by no means all the same thing. Famously, Smith refuses to be side-tracked about the distinction between high and low culture: 'a cultural democracy ... will want to debate the best of everything.' (So Tony Blair entertains Oasis at Number 10 and is a few days later deeply moved by Richard Eyre's *King Lear* at the Cottesloe.) Further, 'just as access and excellence sit together, so too do tradition and innovation. Just because you embrace one does not mean you ditch the other.' And later on, in a list of the purposes of art, Smith celebrates the power of art in cementing community identity, drawing people together, ensuring social inclusion, and overcoming isolation and rejection. However, he also asserts that art is 'not there to make anyone feel warm and cosy; it is there to ask, to probe, to challenge, and to be awkward.'

Cementing community, overcoming isolation, ensuring inclusion. Probing, challenging, being awkward. Of course, to use Smith's favourite formulation, art does *both*. But they are nonetheless different and potentially contradictory objectives. As you can want and achieve both excellence and access. But what if innovative work is inaccessible? If they conflict, where is the priority? After the initial blip of free marketry, the Conservatives were clear about what they wanted culture to do, and the cultural map changed as a result. What different legacy will be left by New Labour, and what is the place of its cultural strategy within the overall project?

In his conclusion to *Cultural Policy and Urban Regeneration: the West European Experience* (from which much of my analysis of urban cultural policy is drawn), co-editor Franco Bianchini suggests how the next stage of urban cultural policy could be different from the three waves which proceeded it. As we move out of the era of utilitarian, economics-led arts strategies, cultural policy may become less about inward investment and more about the redefinition of citizenship. The two key problems faced in this area are indeed 'the increasing social, spatial and cultural segregation of low-income groups' in the cities, and the related need 'to make ethnic and racial minorities an integral part of the civic network'. Certainly, traditional economic and political remedies have failed to solve problems that are too often acquiring the automatic adjective 'intractable'. But by expanding the definition of culture to embrace all aspects of the urban experience (not just recreation, but also architecture, planning, transport and safety), it may be that the arts have a fundamental, practical and urgent task to perform.

These priorities find resonance both in *Creative Britain*, in which Chris Smith celebrates the way (Labour) local authorities in every part of Britain have shown how 'imaginative policies for the arts and cultural activity have an absolutely vital role to play in generating, or regenerating, economic excess and civic pride,' going on to cite Birmingham, Glasgow, Huddersfield and Sheffield in support. In this, he anticipated the first major statement by the new Arts Council chairman Gerry Robinson (Arts Council Annual Lecture, 14 October 1998), which describes in impressive detail a series of examples of projects and endeavours, here and abroad, in which the arts have been popularized both for consumers and participants by projects whose purpose is self-consciously social. From the Los Angeles Philharmonic's strategy to widen its audience base through a multi-cultural repertoire to a plethora of British arts initiatives in areas of deprivation, Robinson advocates the role of the arts in urban rejuvenation, reskilling, strategies for disablement and even healthcare with infectious enthusiasm. As he puts it, it is time 'to review our tendency to see the arts as somehow segregated from the real world ... The truth is the arts *are* the real world.'

Like Chris Smith, Gerry Robinson tends occasionally to indulge in bothism: 'It is not popular art versus high art. It is not art as an economic motor versus art as self-expression. The arts are none of these things and all of these things at the same time.' And his brisk advocacy of 'proper management' and 'sound financing' ignores the catastrophes that have resulted from putting managers and financiers in charge of activities they don't understand.

But the major problem with Robinson's case is the main problem with Labour's cultural strategy and in one sense the main problem with New Labour. The argument is based on the idea that where the interests of the producer and the consumer conflict, then the customer is always right. Thus, Robinson dismisses all too easily the obvious dangers in matching the artistic and indeed political ambitions of producers with utilitarian social need (of which small theatre companies reliant on funding from bodies like the Theatre in Health Education Trust to provide 'service delivery theatre' are all too well aware). Similarly, Robinson's dismissal of George Steiner's argument (in the 1998 Proms lecture) that 'a Philistine, almost vengeful mood is being orchestrated to put in question the role of serious music' underestimates a popular hostility to the unfamiliar and the unconsensual (in form and content) which has resulted from eighteen years of government belligerence towards the provocative and oppositional arts, buttressed by an easy and ill-judged populism from cultural critics who ought to know better. To say that popular and provocative art are not mutually exclusive can easily slide into arguing that if one can swim the other deserves to sink.

In his belief that the market-place can and should reach into areas hitherto dominated by paternalism, Robinson is echoing New Labour's ethos as a whole. If Thatcherism did indeed seek to roll back the supposedly baleful social developments of the 1960s by progressively dismantling the social reforms of the 1940s, then one can see Blairism (and before it Clintonism) as an attempt to detach the 1960s from the 1940s, to pursue the individual ends of the counter-culture while abandoning the more traditional collective means of social democracy, to celebrate the diversity of the new social forces of the 1960s and 1970s at the expense of the challenge they posed to dominant structures, to privilege personal choice over collective action, to validate an individual emotional response to literal and psychological impoverishment while devaluing the conventional structures of political activity, to break the ideological links between oppositional intellectuals and the poor. And the means by which politics might be privatized as lifestyle? Why, by sending it to market. Certainly, let them do their own thing: just not (if you please) in the road.

Hence, surely, Labour's most coherent, best developed and best funded cultural policy. The government's emphasis on access and the money it has put into it makes it a real and proper policy, in stark contradiction to the corporate entertainment ethos of the Thatcher era, and is to be celebrated as such. But by concentrating on the demand side of the equation, it is only half a strategy. On the supply side, the government's most developed innovation the National Endowment for Science, Technology and the Arts (NESTA) – will encourage individual artists but will do little to encourage the institutions in which they will inevitably work. The gradual squeezing out of the oppositional, the daring, the confrontational and the provocative was the aim and achievement of the Conservative government: the paradox is that the healthy and fruitful conversation between patrician traditionalism, market-led populism and provocative artists has always relied on having institutions open to the arguments of all three (such as the pre-Birt BBC). The danger is that this government's proper concern for individual artists and the devolution of power will lead – as it has in broadcasting – to a decline in the attention paid to the overall cultural ecology, within which writers and other artists work throughout their careers. One urgent task of the government is to renew an institutional framework that has been stripped of resources and confidence by the triumph of market populism, in order to create an environment in which the new and the provocative can flourish.

In that, as it happens, it is operating in the most propitious circumstances. For after a long period of easy populism it appears that the arts in general, and the theatre in particular, have gone bolshy again.

Exaggerated deaths: the new writing upsurge of 1992–99

In 1992 I was asked by the British Council to write the text of an exhibition about post-war British playwriting. Comprising twenty-four poster-sized panels on the work of sixty-seven dramatists, the exhibition presented very much the above thesis and, not surprisingly, it ended with more of a whimper than a bang. Looking back on it, and excepting a couple of embarrassingly glaring sins of omission, I would stand by my selection of important playwrights of the 1956 to 1992 period. But in fact the exhibition passed its own sell-by date almost before it was hung. One could now add at least twenty potentially or actually major writers to the list, and via them a fourth act to the three-act story I told.

This remarkable upsurge was enabled by several factors. The first was the opening of two American plays, Tony Kushner's *Angels in America* (opening January 1992) and David Mamet's *Oleanna* (opening in London in October of the same year), which between them goaded the British theatre into remembering a time when British political plays had their finger permanently on the pulse of the times. Second, the popular (and it seems to me rather convenient) view among some directors that playwrights automatically burn out after ten years was disproved by the continuing successes of middle-aged writers: the huge success of the David Hare trilogy at the National demonstrated the continued vibrancy of the state of England play (outperforming as it did *The Recruiting Officer*, *The Seagull* and *A Midsummer Night's Dream* on the Olivier stage), and the continuing inventive vitality of the works of Caryl Churchill confirmed that playwrights over forty are able to keep up with the mercurial advances of cultural theory. Third, the self-help movement among writers themselves – the mushrooming number of organizations, courses and workshops – gave writers an increasing sense of confidence about their craft, a confidence well justified by the structural maturity of plays by writers in their twenties. Fourth, almost all of the young directors of the 1980s who had been so snooty about new writers and their work followed Stephen Daldry away from the antique Spanish Golden Age and towards what increasingly looked like a contemporary British one. Fifth, there was television's virtual abandonment of the single play and its consequent evacuation of territory not visible from a police station, a surgery or the nineteenth century.

But the sixth and main reason is that writers found a subject. Although I understand why writers resist the notion of being part of a movement, it seems to be unanswerable that the mid 1990s had an over-arching theme, embracing gay plays like Jonathan Harvey's *Beautiful Thing* and Kevin Elyot's *My Night with Reg*, boys' bonding plays like Tim Firth's *Neville's Island* (and the boys' betting plays of Patrick Marber and William Gaminara), lads' plays like Jez Butterworth's *Mojo* and Simon Bent's *Goldhawk Rd*, girl-in-a-boys' gang plays like Irving Welsh's *Trainspotting* and Mark Ravenhill's *Shopping and Fucking* (and indeed the subgenre of girls-in-and-out-of-a-boys'-bonding-play, of which genre Terry Johnson's *Dead Funny* remains the market leader). Whatever the distinctions between them, these plays address masculinity and its discontents as demonstrably as the plays of the early 1960s addressed class and those of the 1970s the failures of social democracy. They are once again plays about the unintended consequences of huge social changes, plays which appear about twenty years after great tectonic shifts in the political, cultural and economic geology of the times. The decline of the dominant role of men – in the workplace and in the family – is probably the biggest single story of the last thirty years in the western countries, and it has given a whole generation of young male playwrights – and some women playwrights too – a subject to embrace.

So, five years on from all the obituaries, theatre is listed along with pop, fashion, fine art and food as the fifth leg of the new Swinging London, and not for revivals of de Vega and deconstructions of *A Midsummer Night's Dream*. True, there are some voices still trumpeting the death of the individually written stage play and the final triumph of the site-specific, multi-media, devised, a-linear event, but everyone else is laughing all the way to the Bush. Once again, it seems, theatre has found a subject at the heart of the zeitgeist, and a new generation of directors and actors to realize it. And their collective success is reflected in statistics: up from the single figure percentages of the late 1980s, new work represented over 15 per cent of the repertoire of building-based theatres between 1993 and 1997. Further, its box office performance – below 50 per cent in the late 1980s – rose to 53 per cent in 1993–4 and thence to 57 per cent in 1996–7, outperforming adaptations, post-war revivals, translations, classics and even Shakespeare.

There are, however, some concerns. The first has been expressed by many: it is precisely that the upsurge of new writing is the creation of fashion and may end up its creature. (As Peter Ansorge noted at the 1996 conference 'About Now', the Royal Court's director Stephen Daldry seemed to celebrate this possibility in a London *Evening Standard* interview in early 1997, in which he argued that the wave of gay plays he'd found when he arrived were overtaken first by violent plays and then by the Irish.) Behind the fear of fashion lies a more profound anxiety about the form and content of the new drama.

As stated above, the new stage drama is operating with the context of a British television drama increasingly imprisoned within the homogenizing constraints of genre. Under such circumstances, one might expect theatre to go in the opposite direction. Faced with stylistically predictable, format drama, surely theatre will explode with formal invention. In particular, and following on from current literary and philosophical theory, one would think that theatre makers freed of genre constraints would wish to challenge the linear narrative which is at every genre's core. In fact, almost the reverse has happened. Both *Dead Funny* and *My Night with Reg* positively flaunt their drawing-room-comedy credentials, stage-centre sofa and all; Mark Ravenhill's *Shopping and Fucking* takes place on that very piece of furniture; the published edition of Simon Bent's *Goldhawk Rd* has a sofa *on the front cover*. And the return to plays set in real rooms has been matched by the equally dramatic re-emergence of plays set in real time.

The kitchen-sink drama was so called not just because that's where some of the plays were set, but because they *weren't* set in drawing rooms and country houses, because they *weren't* light social comedies or whodunnits or indeed musical comedies. Superficially, forty years after drama was dragged kicking and screaming from the drawing room into the kitchen, the new generation appears to be dragging it right on back again.

So while the themes of the new plays may be as large as those of the 1980s (for the crisis of masculinity is expressed in violence and suicide; it touches the worlds of education, employment, drugs, sexual politics and crime), their expression is domestic. One might even see the current trend towards autobiographical plays as part of a personalization of the political: Sebastian Barry writes the story of Ireland via that of his family; invited to write about Suez, Christopher Hampton comes up with a play about his childhood; asked to write about Israel, David Hare produces a one-man show.

At 'About Now', Channel 4's former Head of Drama drew on many of these elements of the 1990s upsurge to argue against its importance. For Peter Ansorge, the much-vaunted new wave of contemporary playwriting consists of small-cast pieces of social observation with little narrative and even less to say. There is in this sense no comparison with the golden age of the 1950s and early 1960s when the theatre was indeed in the very eye of the times. And the contemporary plays that *are* any good, like Jez Butterworth's 1950s thriller *Mojo* and Jonathan Harvey's gay romance *Beautiful Thing* – he points out – were all conceived as movies.

When he claims that the plays of today lack narrative, Ansorge may be judging the current new play repertoire a little selectively: Martin McDonagh's plays bristle with narrative, and Conor McPherson has taken storytelling as his form. Further, although there is little prospect of a mass return to the issue plays of the 1970s, there are some young writers, like Michael Punter and David Greig, who are writing about big public questions (particularly the future of Eastern Europe) and will continue to see theatre as a mirror of the public life of the age (Greig sees a stasis at the heart of the *Trainspotting* culture which can only be confronted by plays which go beyond snapshots). While men embrace autobiography, writers like April de Angelis continue not only to write history historically, but to treat the present in the same way. Both Bill Morrison and Anne Devlin, one a Protestant by origin and one a Catholic, feel the weight of the public and private history of Northern Ireland. Like Diane Samuels, Morrison sees the role of theatre as countering the propaganda version: the one thing theatre must do, he argues, is to counter retrospective heroics, and tell you what people really felt about it at the time. Anne Devlin thought she had written out her memories of the near-pogrom of 1969 in Belfast, until she had a child and knew she had to write it again from the perspective of a mother (and an exile). While Conor McPherson, whose father remembers Bloody Sunday for his one-year-old son's whooping cough, insists that 'I will never address that problem in my work', justified by an abiding distrust of the icons of revolutionary patriotism.

And indeed some writers are moving beyond narrative itself, or at least thinking about it in a new way. At 'About Now', David Eldridge challenged the notion that the 'clonky old form of what's-round-the-corner plotting' is the only way to make plays well, in favour of careful character shading, delicate character development and trusting the imaginative impulse. A piece like Rebecca Prichard's 1994 *Essex Girls* appears initially to be no more than two independent slices of life, the first in a girls' school toilet, the second in the high-rise flat of a entrapped young mother. In fact, the geometry of the play – the first act an energetic trio between three schoolgirls waiting for the sole usable lavatory cubicle to become free, the second a dialogue between the monosyllabic young mother and her chaotically and desperately prolix friend – is a vivid metaphor not just for what will happen to the three girls of the first act but how it will happen (with an unexpected twist at the end providing a hint of how it might be different). The work of Phyllis Nagy, too, demands that the audience find meaning in distinctions and rupture as well as continuity. Another example is Martin Crimp's *Attempts on Her Life*, presented by the Royal Court in

1997, in which a series of apparently disconnected groups and individuals describe what we are invited to think of as a single woman called Anne, possessed nonetheless of various nationalities, histories and ages, who appears at one point to be a terrorist (of left or right), at another the drowned daughter of grieving parents, at another an artist and even a newly launched car. Crimp's purpose is not only to question whether we can truly know another human being, but whether we can regard other people as existing at all independent of the models we construct of them. And he does this not by a bald statement, but by playing an elaborate and sophisticated game with the audience's expectations of how scenes connect within narrative.

So it may be that precisely at the moment when television, radio and film drama are rushing pell-mell back towards the certainties of traditional, genre-based narrative forms, new British playwrights are finding ways to challenge the assumptions of traditional storytelling, without losing the accessibility which has always been the British theatre's particular virtue.

Despite the stature of individual figures like Osborne, Pinter, Stoppard, Bond, Ayckbourn, Hare and Churchill, the success of British playwriting of the last forty years has not been merely a matter of individual genius. It has been about providing a forum in which a succession of writers can speak seriously about the times to an audience which shares their obsessions, their concerns and their language. And it seems clear that, once again, a new generation of British playwrights has found a subject and a form in which to address it, as acutely and potentially more subtly than their peers in the other storytelling media.

And if, as I have argued, the women writers of the 1980s were the third wave of a rolling conversation about cultural emancipation which had begun with *Look Back in Anger* and *Roots*, it is possible that their work provided the opening statement of a new cycle of exploration. If the initiating event of the theatre of Osborne and Wesker was the Second World War, then the theatre movement that begins with the late 1970s work of Pam Gems and Caryl Churchill surely responds to the women's liberation movement of the late 1960s. In this reading, the current crop of men-unravelling plays is stage two of this conversation; another group of young playwrights anatomizing the fallout of a huge tectonic shift in the political, cultural and economic geology of the times.

The Bush's director Mike Bradwell argues that theatre needs to recapture its sense of the seriousness of its own mission. Faced with the fashionable contempt of those cultural critics who find theatre too much like hard work, theatre should celebrate rather than downplay the moral rigour of its endeavour, and return to its primary purpose of examining 'who we are and why we do what we do'. Since 1956, each individual wave of the cycle has offered a different answer to the second question. While perhaps the underlying subject of the cycle as a whole is not what we do but who we are.

Then and now

At 'About Now', Nicholas Wright listed a number of enemies of new writing, of which the most surprising was Englishness. It was there because, as a South African, Wright had now found an identity with the country of his birth – its institutions, its anthem, its flag – which he felt was not available to English writers. For most contemporary playwrights, British national identity has been a subject of external observation. As Viktor Shklovsky wrote, 'theatre's colour has not tended to reflect the colour of the flag that waves over the fortress of the city.'

But perhaps this reflects a narrow view of both nation and identity. Up until 1956, Britain's sense of its national identity was dominated by three certainties: what we had been before the war, what we became during it, and a vision of what we would become in the future. All of those certainties were challenged in 1956: the Suez fiasco undermined both the pre-war imperial heritage and the moral assurance of the anti-fascist war; Krushschev's condemnation of Stalin (and subsequent suppression of the Hungarian revolution) destroyed any remaining illusions about our wartime ally, and undermined post-war hopes of a socialist future. From the year of *Look Back in Anger* on, post-imperial Britishness was of itself a problematic concept.

Because our borders have not been in contest (on the mainland at least), it is easy to lose sight of the national dimension of the struggle for identity which has, in its myriad ways, underlined the conversation in the theatre from 1956 to now. Clearly, as Wright points out, Osborne was obsessed with Englishness; Hare, Brenton, Churchill and Wertenbaker (among others) pose political questions in national language. And in celebration of the feminist company Monstrous

Regiment (at the 1998 conference 'Better Red'), Gillian Hanna emphasized its place in the political culture 'of this country'.

During 'National Stages', any easy conclusions about the political colour of nationalism came under challenge. East European speakers in no doubt of the importance of nationalism to their escape from the Soviet empire were nonetheless embarrassed by a nationhood expressed in ersatz recreations of doubtful provenance. Anatoly Smelyansky of the Moscow Arts Theatre clearly welcomed the demise of the socialist realist play in which the wise old party boss knew all the answers; he was less sure about the current flush of plays in which the progressive collective farm worker is elbowed out by the progressive kulak, the heroic White Guard is substituted for the heroic Red commissar, and 'the chap playing Lenin yesterday, plays Nicholas II today.' Nigerian writer and academic Femi Osofisan defined the nation as 'what we know when we do not ask about it', a definition that becomes both more ambivalent and more interesting in view of his reminder that all nations are man-made structures, and his own nation more man-made than most. Richard Gough (of Cardiff's Centre for Performance Research) reminded the conference that 'Welsh national costume' was invented in the nineteenth century.

Of course everyone shares Yvonne Brewster's quizzical response to seeing African weaving hung in a frame, a doomed attempt 'to constrain the essentially fluid and tactile'. But her call for 'bold new hybrids' begs the question of what is being hyphenated and thus transformed. Both Bill Morrison and Christina Reid come from Northern Ireland Protestant backgrounds: Reid's grandfather once told her, 'Your problem is, you don't know who you are'; while Morrison's response to the Bloody Sunday massacre in 1972 was to renounce his British citizenship and voluntarily redefine himself as a member of 'what was then one of the socially most repressive regimes in Europe'. The question of who we are – whether, as Winsome Pinnock ruefully put it, she is a woman playwright, a black woman playwright or just a playwright – is also the question of who we belong to.

How communities of difference relate not just within themselves but between each other in an increasingly globalized but also fractured world is the major human question we'll confront in the new century. Because it is an essentially cultural question (as opposed to the questions posed by traditional Marxism or entrepreneurial liberalism), the question of belonging will inevitably foreground the arts, and particularly the narrative arts, as people seek ever more desperately to construct, deconstruct and reassemble stories that make sense of the world. British theatre has survived the last forty-five years because with considerable seriousness, in literal conversation with its audience, it has faced up to the question of how our various, myriad and contradictory affinities, histories and identities relate to each other. It has provided the most consistently effective platform for a series of challenges to both the patrician and the populist conceptions of class and gender roles, sexuality and nationhood. In that sense, if it has fulfilled one task above all others, it has been to provoke.

Long may it so remain.

David Edgar founded the MA course in playwriting studies at the University of Birmingham and convened the Birmingham Theatre Conference from 1990 to 1999. His stage plays include *Destiny* (RSC, 1976), an adaptation of *Nicholas Nickleby* (RSC, 1980), *Maydays* (RSC, 1983), *The Summer* (Hampstead Theatre, 1987), *The Shape of the Table* (National Theatre, 1990), and *Pentecost* (RSC, 1994–5), which won the *Evening Standard* Award for best play. His work for the BBC includes *Buying a Landslide* (BBC2, 1992) and *Talking to Mars* (Radio 3, 1996).

PART TWO

About Now

Extracts from the Birmingham Theatre Conferences
'About Now' and 'Reality Time'

Really a Golden Age?

Peter Ansorge

When I first arrived there were a lot of gay plays, then came
violent plays like *Mojo* and *Shopping and Fucking*. I feel that
trend is on the way out now. The next big wave to crash will be
Irish writing.
Stephen Daldry, artistic director of the Royal Court Theatre, London *Evening
Standard*, 10 January 1997

I tend to go to film previews during the day. In the States recently I
saw *Mars Attacks!* Tim Burton has done a great job portraying
youthful irony and subverting it cleverly. *Rita, Sue and Bob Too*,
Trainspotting and *Pulp Fiction* are three of my all-time favourites –
these films tell it like it is. I love anything that's shocking to safe,
Home Counties folk and pushes back the boundaries.
Wayne Hemingway, co-founder of Red or Dead fashion label, *Guardian*,
21 February 1997

These two statements reveal a great deal about our 'cultural life' but
not in the way that either speaker perhaps intended. Stephen Daldry
was answering a question posed by journalists to artists from time
immemorial. Could Daldry, asked the *Evening Standard*'s Michael
Owen, spot any *trends* among playwrights today? What is interesting
is not so much Daldry's reply but the enthusiasm with which he
embraces the whole idea of a trend in the theatre. It is possible that a
seventeenth-century hack might have asked a similar question of
Shakespeare and even been provided with an answer of sorts.
('Danes are out, dear boy, but the Scots are definitely in.') Yet I
very much doubt it. What is true is that none of Daldry's predecessors
at the Court – Stafford-Clark, Gaskill, Lindsay Anderson or Tony
Richardson – would have given the *Evening Standard*'s question any
serious consideration at all. They were in the business of bucking
trends – of supporting writers over a number of productions or in the

case of Osborne and Beckett, even decades. Fashionable labels like 'kitchen-sink drama' were loathed, not loved, by the practitioners in Sloane Square. They were the enemies of art, which defines fashion in a way that is often beyond the comprehension of journalists.

Wayne Hemingway strikes a similar note to Daldry's in the *Guardian*. *Trainspotting* and *Pulp Fiction* were major influences behind the first-wave successes of Daldry at the Court. Yet these works have not been shocking audiences all over the Home Counties, as Hemingway implies, either as plays or films. They are carefully targeted pieces that appeal to and flatter a young audience where the drug culture now has the widest possible acceptance. The Home Counties crowd who might indeed be shocked by such works simply do not go and see them. We are living through a time when people are turning away from controversial drama rather than embracing it. The kids go to *Trainspotting* and their parents to *Sense and Sensibility*.

The recent work at the Court cannot compare with the impact of *Look Back in Anger* or the Wesker Trilogy in the 1950s. Then, shocked faces from the Home Counties *did* interweave with the angry features of the young. Rows broke out about plays during intervals. Peter Hall tells the story that after the first night of *Waiting for Godot* at the Arts Theatre in 1955 half the audience cheered and the other half booed. As a sixth-former in London during the early 1960s I saw Arnold Wesker's *Chips with Everything* at the Royal Court and will never forget its climax. An indictment of national service, the play ends on a note of bitter irony with *God Save the Queen* being performed by the whole cast. In those days every performance in the theatre *had* to end with the national anthem being played and the audience standing up in respect. At the end of *Chips with Everything*, half of those in the packed auditorium rose to their feet in order to salute the Queen while the other half remained stubbornly seated. I really did see a lady in a blue hat quarrelling with a young man who refused to rise, it seemed to me, in wonder at the play. The woman encouraged the young man by lashing out at him with her umbrella, but without success. Who knows – it might have been the young David Hare or David Edgar.

Writers and directors work in a very different climate today. There is no going back to the heady days of the 1950s and 1960s, when people really did believe – perhaps naïvely – that the individual voice of a playwright could set the cultural agenda for an entire nation. But it does seem to me that the authors of *Look Back in Anger* and *Waiting for Godot* benefited immensely from the lack of anything in the London of their day that might be even remotely described as fringe theatre. For the fact remains that since the late 1970s new plays in this country have been premiered almost exclusively in small auditoria or pub theatres. The Royal Court's Theatre Upstairs, the Bush, Hampstead Theatre Club, the National's Cottesloe and the Royal Shakespeare Company's tiny Pit have been the main platforms for launching the best new work.

This has meant that the majority of the work has been written for small spaces with tiny casts. The Bush and Theatre Upstairs in particular have pioneered a style of playwriting that is economical in the extreme. Short scenes, time and place fragmented by swift lighting changes, the minimum of scenery: a new play culture has emerged that at times can appear hermetically sealed off from the outside. This is in direct contrast to the birth of fringe theatre some thirty years ago, which came out in active opposition to the work being presented at the National, Royal Court or RSC. Actors, directors and writers became involved in the fringe as a first step – or so they imagined – to storming the citadels of the larger subsidized companies or even the West End. The fringe has now become an end in itself, practically the only producer of new writing. If it still represents radicalism of a kind in the theatre, then it is an entirely marginalized rebellion.

The artistic confinement has, in my view, affected the nature of the plays. The central vision has become small-scale. In this respect Max Stafford-Clark's regime at the Royal Court during the 1980s is significant. Apart from Caryl Churchill's work, there were few first nights that could compete with the finest memories of previous regimes. The majority of plays ran for very limited seasons, with a huge reliance on favourable notices in *Time Out* to gain any kind of audience at all. They increasingly appealed to audiences who merely wanted their political prejudices confirmed. The profile of new writing began to change. There was nothing to compare with the public debate surrounding Osborne and Wesker's work under George Devine and Tony Richardson; no innovation of style or content that could compete with William Gaskill's early direction of Edward Bond or with Lindsay Anderson's impeccable productions of David Storey's work plays.

In his revealing introduction to a compilation of recent Bush Theatre plays, the departing artistic director Dominic Dromgoole writes: 'Although it's the last thing people would say of the Bush, it's actually more of a European than a British theatre, in the sense of its understanding of stories. Many theatres are crushed by the heavy hand of the twentieth century British tradition ... This is the theatre of thumping "boys-own" plots and big noisy messages.'

Dromgoole goes on to say that a typical Bush play is 'more glancing, oblique, opaque. Life and truth matter more in the Bush than point or suspense.' It is true that the plays in Dromgoole's collection do not address public issues or stylistic ambition a great deal. But neither do they seem particularly 'European' in their presentation of character. The plays seem to be very recognizable pieces of British fringe theatre today. Much of the writing of the characters is indeed witty and truthful – but it does not represent a return to narrative among younger writers. The Bush plays contain almost no narrative to enforce a piece of on-stage action.

This does not mean that all plays require vast amounts of on-stage action to succeed. Jonathan Harvey's *Beautiful Thing* – a Bush discovery – was a kind of gay update of Shelagh Delaney's 1950s hit *A Taste of Honey* (in which a pregnant working-class girl poignantly befriends a homosexual). The comic power of *Beautiful Thing* stemmed entirely from its beautifully observed insights into the reality of coming out on a council estate. Yet the actual structure of the play is even more anecdotal than *A Taste of Honey*.

While the Bush has been encouraging writers to lower their public voices, the new regime at the Court has been cultivating a post-Thatcher brat-pack of writers in their early twenties who are un-doubtedly in touch with the mood of young audiences. Under Stephen Daldry's regime there has been a welcome effort to commission a new generation of writers to produce plays for and about the young. In Nick Grosso's *Peaches*, the anti-hero Frank announces to his friend Johnny: 'There's no point in being old and saying you lived a little, talking about the war – you gotta talk about *babes* when you're old, tell your grandkids all about it. Fuck the fucking war!'

Frank's existence in *Peaches* is entirely governed by his relations with 'babes'. The scenes wittily consist of him talking to one girl about another – and then cutting to him in the presence of the new girl. The play is an engaging round of male chat-up and eventual disappoint-ment. Alongside Grosso, writers like Michael Wynne and Rebecca Prichard have been presenting audiences with some cool assessments of their tribes. Much of the writing focuses on the personal lives of the characters – their struggles to find love and understanding in a recession-hit Britain which seems to pay them little heed. In general the plays are strong on dialogue but have virtually no plots at all. In comparison, the first generation of Royal Court writers in the 1950s began with major, not minor, work. Perhaps because they had experience of a world war and a Britain that was beginning to take notice of the young, writers like Osborne and Wesker could produce work on a much broader canvas.

When the new writers do turn to narrative, the main influences often come from film and television. Jez Butterworth's feisty encounter with a 1950s Soho underworld, *Mojo*, in fact began life as a screenplay and is one of the few new plays in recent years to be written with 'suspense and point' rather than out of a desire to describe a series of relationships. As an exercise in style, *Mojo* is breathtaking, evoking a gruesome society of its own imagining. The action unfolds exactly like a Tarantino thriller – with a group of tragi-comic gangsters playing out the brutal consequences of a crime. It was a startling début that only begged the question of the point of it all. *Mojo* is telling us nothing new about Soho in the 1950s. It is purely an effective location for a series of violent actions that delighted a predominantly young audience weaned on *Reservoir Dogs*.

The fact that both *Beautiful Thing* and *Mojo* were originally conceived as film scripts rather than stage plays does suggest a change in priorities for the new generation of playwrights. From *Look Back in Anger* to *The Absence of War* we have turned to the stage for entertaining plays that are also important commentaries on British society. That model seems increasingly irrelevant to younger playwrights.

Curiously, newspapers and magazines would have us believe differently. Michael Billington and Benedict Nightingale have both gone on record recently to argue that British theatre is going through a golden age of new writing. 'I cannot recall', stated Billington in the *Guardian* (13 March 1996), 'a time when there were so many exciting dramatists in the twentysomething age-group: what is more, they seem to be speaking to audiences of their own generation.' He cited new plays by Jez Butterworth, the late Sarah Kane and David Eldridge among others. Benedict Nightingale's list of new playwrights (*The Times*, 1 May 1996) included Kane and Butterworth, but went on to praise works by such names as Simon Bent, Joe Penhall and Judy Upton. Nightingale's article began with a reference to Tom Stoppard: 'Tom Stoppard once said he became a playwright because John Osborne's *Look Back in Anger* caused such a stir that the theatre was clearly "the place to be at". There is a similar buzz in the air now ...' Except that there isn't, unless you happen to work in theatre. No one would wish to detract from the promise of Butterworth or Grosso. But their works are not known to the general public in the way that John Osborne's *Look Back in Anger* or Arnold Wesker's *Roots* were in the 1950s. There is no real debate about the new plays or their subject matter. They do not seem to suggest the kind of metaphor that might get an audience, beyond a specific age group, actually talking about their content and meaning. There is a vague feeling on the part of critics that young people are becoming interested in theatre again, which of course we all welcome. But they insist that new young writers should command our interest without ever explaining why. Nightingale is almost apologetic about his enthusiasm: 'All have had premières at the Royal Court and its Theatre Upstairs or at the Bush Theatre ... unlike the dramatists that preceded them, these writers have no obvious political credo, no social agenda, and take a quizzical view of human nature.'

In other words, unlike Osborne, Pinter, Shaffer, Brenton or Hare, these new writers have almost nothing to say. If 'a quizzical view of human nature' had been the only platform for championing Osborne or Beckett during the 1950s, absolutely no one would have turned up at the box office. Billington and Nightingale make almost no reference to the actual content of the new plays – a new way of storytelling that might attract us, characters which will move or excite us. In the past, these critics have given Hare and Stoppard a far fiercer grilling than they have ever served up for Butterworth or Penhall. Yet theatre critics now assume that their readers will support a culture of new writing purely for its own sake. As the profile of new writing declines, as the impact on a mainstream audience collapses, so the call to *support* new writing intensifies.

During the past few years the BBC has practically killed off the viewer's appetite for new writing and the single play by presenting an interminably depressing series of one-off films under the *Screen Two* label on Saturday nights. Week after week we were presented with the bleakest portraits of life in Britain that have probably ever been conceived, which were then written and directed in the most depressing way imaginable. As a tale of incest in the inner city followed a bloody account of drug taking in the inner city so the BBC announcer would prepare us for the subject matter of next week's film – a harrowing account of homelessness in the inner city. Many of the films were praised by the television critics and picked up awards around the world. Yet because they cost on average around £800,000 per hour, the BBC started to panic when audience figures fell below a million viewers.

Obviously our business needs to attract new talent – neither theatre nor television will survive without the young coming in. But to make a fetish of new writing when plays themselves have only a marginal appeal to audiences is a self-defeating exercise. Audiences will not pay for a seat at the box office or turn on a play on television simply because it is a worthy thing to do. No one wishes to take anything away from the importance of the work currently being produced at the Bush Theatre or the Royal Court's Theatre Upstairs. But it is critical tomfoolery to suggest that a new *Look Back in Anger* is being discovered each month. There is in fact no evidence that every generation produces dramatists of real distinction. Greek tragedy and comedy flourished for about seventy years, the Elizabethan and Jacobean theatres for an even shorter span of time. There is little reason to believe that the movement begun by George Devine and Tony Richardson in 1956 will necessarily last for ever.

The mid 1980s saw the emergence of a very talented crop of new directors in British theatre. Yet Deborah Warner, Declan Donnellan, Stephen Pimlott, Matthew Warchus, Phyllida Lloyd, Stephen Daldry and Sam Mendes all won their reputations through classical revivals or with plays and musicals from previous decades. They are Thatcher's children in the theatre, not on a political but on an aesthetic plane. None is closely identified with a contemporary writer in the tradition of Tony Richardson and John Osborne, John Dexter and Arnold Wesker, Peter Hall and Harold Pinter, Peter Wood and Tom Stoppard, Lindsay Anderson and David Storey, William Gaskill and Edward Bond or Richard Eyre and David Hare.

It is true that Phyllida Lloyd has directed both Terry Johnson and John Guare at the Royal Court, but she won her spurs at the National with the classics. Declan Donnellan directed *Angels in America* at the National, but he is best known as the creator of Cheek By Jowl, who of course specialise in revivals. In the way that spectacle in the past decade dominated the West End theatre through *Cats*, *Phantom* and *Starlight Express*, so it did our subsidized stages. Daldry's *An Inspector Calls* and Warchus's *Volpone* were undoubtedly stunning theatrical events – evoking a Thatcherite obsession with private capital and greed in both J. B. Priestley's London and Ben Jonson's Venice. But the audience went away from those shows if not (in Michael Billington's memorable phrase about Lloyd Webber musicals) 'humming the sets' then certainly thinking as much about them as the plays. Deborah Warner was taken to task by the *Guardian* for confessing that she won't direct plays by living writers because they are always 'neurotic'. In reply she stated that 'I would love to direct a new play when there are new plays of the size that is offered to me in classics ... one you could give a year of your life to.'

In *Power Play,* Stephen Fay's biography of Peter Hall, it's mentioned that in 1953 West End managers commissioned and financed twenty-six new plays, a number that is inconceivable today, when stars cannot be tempted to commit to long runs and directors like Deborah Warner might demand a year's rehearsal period. In 1953, of course, most of those twenty-six plays would have had common settings with characters from exclusively middle-class and upper-middle-class backgrounds. As Kenneth Tynan wrote of the typical play of the day: 'The setting is in a country house in what used to be called Loamshire, but now, as a heroic tribute to realism, is sometimes called Berkshire.' We now look back on those days with a smile of superiority. Yet writers then held a far more powerful position in West End theatre than is the case today. There was a greater variety of new work being presented, properly resourced and managed. It is for these reasons that younger directors may prefer to revive Rattigan, Coward or Priestley than to have to depend on a pub environment in which to present new plays by their peers. Certainly they do not seem to be giving writers the kind of resources that a classic play now commands.

From the mid 1950s to the late 1970s the Royal Court was unquestionably the primary home of the best new writing talent. It was also the first port of call for many of our best directors. Meanwhile, at the Royal Shakespeare Company, Harold Pinter was the company's number two house dramatist. The National Theatre had Peter Nichols and the young Tom Stoppard as their stars in the new writing firmament. Our three strongest subsidized theatres therefore championed different writers but also competing directorial styles. The Court favoured plain white lighting on stage with minimalist sets drawn from raw materials like steel and leather, of which the designer Jocelyn Herbert was the great pioneer. The RSC built on this style for their productions of both Shakespeare and Pinter. Under Olivier, the National Theatre developed a far more baroque and catholic approach to design and production. The three theatres clung fiercely to their separate artistic identities. When Peter Hall's name was mentioned as the successor to Olivier at the National, Kenneth Tynan protested to the Board that 'We are the Cavaliers, Stratford the Roundheads – with the emphasis on analytic intelligence and textual clarity. Under Peter Hall the country would have two Roundhead theatres.' At the same time, a flourishing fringe theatre was producing new writing responsive to the student movement and political questioning of the late 1960s.

During the 1980s each of these theatres, including the fringe, lost their identities as far as new writing was concerned. With certain exceptions, such as David Hare at the National and Caryl Churchill at the Court, writers were no longer identified with the policies of an individual theatre or director. In fact, there were no artistic policies because, as Eliza Doolittle's father says of morals, theatres could no longer afford them. Directors went where the work was – not to a building that represented an idea of what theatre ought to be. New writing was in any case confined to small spaces with tiny casts. Yet ambitious design and epic staging had been a crucial factor behind the success of post-war British playwrights, from Osborne's *Luther* at the Court to Shaffer's *Royal Hunt of the Sun* and *Amadeus* at the National. Peter Hall's large-scale productions of Pinter's work at the RSC would have been unthinkable without the breadth of designer John Bury's visual imagination. Few who saw the original production of Pinter's *The Homecoming* in the 1960s can forget the choice of furniture, let alone the writing and acting. New writing rarely offers a director this kind of opportunity today. It is for this reason that they have largely abandoned new writing in favour of spectacular productions of the classics and musicals.

For it is the rise of the British musical that has been the real event of the last twenty years. From *Cats* to *Evita* and *Sunset Boulevard*, Andrew Lloyd Webber and his collaborators have created a sense of spectacle and occasion with which the public now automatically associates a good night out. The majority of playwrights cannot compete and probably would not wish to. Like most people, I have taken children to performances of *Cats* and been hugely entertained. I remember looking at the young audiences who flocked to *Evita* in the late 1970s – when there were only two other musicals playing in the West End – and thinking that Hal Prince's kitsch but memorable production had done a great service to the theatre by bringing in audiences who normally only attended rock concerts or pantomimes. I had failed to see that Lloyd Webber's singular achievement was to have combined these two previously distinct genres. Audiences the world over, not merely on Broadway, now look upon theatre primarily as a place to see musicals.

Watching Stephen Daldry's production of *An Inspector Calls*, one is aware of a design concept comparable to that of *The Phantom of the Opera*. Without it, you doubt whether Daldry would have been interested in reviving the play. The house that visibly crumbled on stage equals the shock of the chandelier that the Phantom sends hurtling down on the audience just before the interval of Lloyd Webber's musical. Such resources have simply not been given to new plays during this period. The profile of new writing has suffered as a result. It is also possible that working on new plays requires a different approach.

Despite a so-called golden age of new writing currently taking place in the theatre, most young playwrights are actually hard at work at their screenplays. Jez Butterworth and Jonathan Harvey first thought of *Mojo* and *Beautiful Thing* as feature films rather than stage plays. Ironically, the success of both in the theatre gave them the chance to write the screenplays. It is to Los Angeles – or failing that, Channel 4 – that young writers look for the future rather than Sloane Square or Shaftesbury Avenue. Interestingly, the majority have complete con-tempt for television drama. The opportunity to address a national audience through popular drama – so relished by Dennis Potter, Alan Bleasdale, Ken Loach and Jimmy McGovern – has little appeal. Yet movies remain a director's medium, not a writer's. Paula Milne's Channel 4 serial *The Politician's Wife* will always be associated with her authorship. Yet her screenplay *The Hollow Reed* which the channel commissioned in the same year became known as 'a film by Angela Pope'. British directors like Jon Amiel and Mick Jackson who have left for Hollywood now produce far worse work there than they once did for the BBC and Channel 4. Those who remain under the umbrella of British television keep on getting better.

In *A Dance to the Music of Time*, the novelist Anthony Powell describes the presence of talent in his generation as at once its most vulnerable and yet most robust characteristic. Given the right circumstances, the writer can become one of the most bloody-minded of survivors. It was the Royal Court in the 1950s that first gave playwrights a chance to be at the centre of the dramatic process. Here was a theatre in which acting, direction and lighting were all subservient to the intentions of the script. A generation of directors – Tony Richardson, Lindsay Anderson, William Gaskill and John Dexter – all took their first inspiration from the text. Nuance, texture, meaning and a fundamental simplicity (by no means simple to achieve) became the primary objectives in the staging of any new play. This did not mean that the directors were minor figures in the productions. Dexter ran his productions with military precision, often instilling fear and trembling into the actors and writer, until his highest ambitions were achieved. Anderson and Gaskill were notorious for their waspish sensibilities and dominant personalities. Yet their talents were primarily given over to the interpretation of a text. The influence of this work spread way beyond the Royal Court's smallish theatre in Sloane Square. It gained a world-wide reputation for the theatre's writers and actors as well as the directors. It paved the way for a generation of television directors to work on scripts in a similar way, particularly on the BBC's 'Play for Today' strand in the 1960s and 1970s. The British directors who are currently lauded in Hollywood won their spurs during that spring of television drama. It was truly a golden age.

Does anyone feel equally confident about today?

Peter Ansorge is executive producer with the BBC's independent commissioning group, currently producing projects by Paula Milne and Alan Bleasdale. He began his career at the BBC, where his commissions included David Hare's *Licking Hitler* and the series *Gangsters* and *Empire Road*. From 1987 he was responsible for commissioning drama serials and series at Channel 4, where his award-winning commissions included *A Very British Coup*, *GBH*, *Lipstick On Your Collar* and *The Politician's Wife*. He is the author of *Disrupting the Spectacle*, a book about fringe theatre in Britain in the 1970s, and his account of writing for theatre, television and film today (*From Liverpool to Los Angeles*) was published in 1997 by Faber and Faber.

Plays about Men

Mark Ravenhill, Kevin Elyot, William Gaminara

Mark Ravenhill

> Ever since I started work in the theatrical profession I have tried to attack the dominance of homosexuals in all its fields ... It seems to me that most homosexual art tends to be – or at least to become – over traditional, conservative, narrow, parochial, self congratulatory, narcissistic. The English theatre has been dominated by highly talented homosexuals. The result is stagnation in the form of unreal chintzy plays, gorgeous décor and a glamorous selection of theatrical lords and ladies. I detest this kind of theatre and all things it represents and defends and I shall go on attacking it because it is bad, boring and unadventurous art. If heterosexual art is better, let us produce some.
> Letter to the *Daily Express*, 11 April 1959

In the *Daily Express* of 10 April 1959, John Deane Potter reported the fining of John Cranko, co-author of the spectacularly successful revue *Cranks*, for a crime known as 'the West End Vice'. Now in this day and age we may have an altogether different definition of the West End Vice – maybe a strange compulsion to present musicals compiled from the back catalogue of rock and pop artistes – but in 1959 the *Daily Express* meant cottaging.

Cranko's cottaging conviction led the *Daily Express* to berate the theatre as 'full of people belonging to a secret brotherhood ... tortured misfits', and, lest we miss the point, 'they are evil.' The article continued: 'What is often received with trills of praise by the closed West End set remains puzzling to the normal mind of the average theatregoer who is unaware of the lace-like intricacies of the decor or the obscure oddities of the plot. And the theatre has an expensive flop on its hands.'

Producers beware, heed the *Daily Express*. Homosexuals lose you money.

The next day, the *Express* printed a response from a young playwright who, while he disagreed with Potter's suggestion that homosexuals should be driven from their positions of theatrical power, went on to argue that the influence of homosexuals in the English theatre had led to a stagnated, detestable, boring and unadventurous art. The young playwright was John Osborne, and his words are telling for two reasons.

Firstly, in a minor way, because Osborne's sexuality was itself unsettled. He admitted to being 'thirty per cent queer'. But also, more significantly, because it makes us rethink the classic narrative handed down to us that theatre was in a parlous state before the arrival of Osborne and the boys at the Court, and that they waded in and sorted out the mess. While this narrative has been classically told in class terms – snobby Coward and Rattigan swept aside by the grammar-school meritocracy of the Court – looked at in terms of sexuality the narrative is more complex. The mincing old poofs – Noel, Terry, Binkie, Johnnie, Ralphie – were being pushed aside by the Angry Straight Young Men. Of course, although the new writers were straight, many of the Court's directors were queer and so they invented a new puritan aesthetic for directing and design to distance themselves as firmly as they could from the chintz and gorgeous décor Osborne so decried.

Cultural commentators always seem to welcome those moments in our cultural life when the white boys are sent in to sort everything out. Just when a combination of blacks and queens, and quite a few black queens, had invented disco, along came the white boys with guitars to give us punk and make it all real again. And just when the tastes of teenage girls and gay men had saturated the market with boy bands, along came the lads of Oasis and Blur to give us real music, and the narrative is written that trashy, silly music is replaced with the real thing. As someone who enjoys 'Relight My Fire' more than 'Wonderwall', I beg to differ.

It seems to me that a similar thing has been happening recently in the theatre. Following the success of Kushner, Harvey et al, the cry goes up from the media: thank God, the boys are back in town – Grosso, Penhall, Marber, etc etc etc, are here to butch it all up, to make it real, to make it vigorous, just like it was in the 1950s. An injection of testosterone and we'll be OK again.

What we have been suffering recently is a plague of straight boys' plays on the London stage. Large numbers of men and women – gay and straight – have paid considerable amounts of money to see these plays. I think the reasons for this are complex, but here are a couple of thoughts. We're now more comfortable about objectifying the male body in a way that we used only to do with women's bodies. Straight men and women will now acknowledge that one of the pleasures of theatre is checking out the totty on stage.

More seriously, I would suggest that the all-male and the gay play or the all-male gay play have been popular because there is a crisis in heterosexuality. So deep are the suspicions and tensions between heterosexual men and women that it is almost impossible to stage their relationships. The male and female part of our psyches are pushing further and further apart and to bring them together on stage can only result in a huge conflict, a conflict that only David Mamet in *Oleanna* has dared to stage.

The boys' play has always been with us and will probably always be with us. But we can probably trace its rebirth in recent times to the all-boys *Glengarry Glen Ross*, one of my Desert Island Plays. It opens in a Chinese restaurant and with its overlapping dialogues and hyper-realistic speech it reinvents theatrical language. It then moves into an office and explores the corrupting influence of market forces on language, morality and humanity. It was written within a year of *Top Girls*, another of my Desert Island Plays. This opens in a restaurant and with its overlapping dialogues and hyper-realistic speech it reinvents theatrical language. It moves into an office and explores the corrupting influence of market forces on language, morality and humanity. Spooky, huh? Why then has Mamet's been followed by scores of all-male plays and Churchill's by only a handful of all-girl?

Some contemporary gay practitioners have recently aligned them-selves with the gay tradition so rudely interrupted by the Court in the 1950s, particularly Neil Bartlett (whose *Night After Night* celebrated the homosexual subtext of classic West End shows) or Sean Mathias with his 'rediscovery' of *Design for Living*. I don't feel as able to embrace this rather camp tradition as Neil or Sean, but you can imagine I am wary of throwing my hat in with the 'butch' tradition of the Royal Court.

Writing plays is far too difficult for me to concern myself with fulfilling any theoretical notions while I'm writing them. I do know that I don't want to write gay plays, because I'm not that keen on being a 'gay man'. As a construct, 'gay' has now been wholly appropriated as a consumer label, not as a political definition of oneself. A couple of years ago, radical gay men tried calling themselves 'queer' but that always felt a bit silly, so for the moment I'd probably call myself 'post-gay', at least until something better comes along. 'Gay theatre' has become 'Calvin theatre' – so called because of the underwear so proudly and prominently displayed by its protagonists – which often seems as self-congratulatory and narcissistic as Osborne said it would be.

Kevin Elyot

I'm wary of trends, suspecting the wrong conclusion can be drawn from what is sometimes an arbitrary set of circumstances. For example, when my play *My Night with Reg* was produced in the West End, there were one or two other plays around with gay characters. It was pure chance they happened to overlap, but we were subjected to a little flurry of newspaper articles about a plague of pink plays. The writing process, as everyone knows, can be a very isolated business, and when you finally emerge into the light, hoping that what you've written might be of some interest to somebody after all those months of mental solitary confinement, it can come as a bit of a surprise to be told that quite a few other writers have written the same sort of thing and that you are part of a trend. So, after the pink-play-plague trend, I now find myself unwittingly part of the blokes-in-a-room trend.

All I would offer as a starting point is a brief explanation of why I wrote about boys in a room. The boys side of things speaks for itself. The reason *My Night with Reg* consists only of men, and exclusively gay men, is that I felt it was through these characters that I could express myself most honestly. It was actually commissioned by Hampstead Theatre – and turned down by them too, one of the reasons being that they felt it was too hermetically sealed. I didn't agree. A play can create the tiniest, most esoteric world and if it's well enough done I think it will resonate with no problem.

As for rooms, it depends what's happening in them. There are three reasons why *My Night with Reg* is set in a drawing room (with french windows, no less). First of all, it serves the time trick of the play: it's in three scenes – late afternoon, dusk and dawn – and on one level the action could seem to be taking place over the course of a single evening, but eventually one realizes that there are huge leaps in time, and setting all the action in the same room helps to pull this off.

Secondly, I like the idea of the set suggesting a boulevard comedy but then subverting the genre in that it's about men desiring each other, having each other, betraying each other and dying. And thirdly, I wanted to set myself the challenge of writing sustained scenes, not using filmic cuts, but following the example of Chekhov or Ibsen, a play revealing itself over three or four movements.

Finally, I would add that my new play for the National (*The Day I Stood Still*) is also set in a drawing room, but things happen to the room and this time it's not peopled exclusively with boys.

William Gaminara

I worked in the early 1980s for an organization called MEND – Members of Equity for Nuclear Disarmament – and I wrote a load of sketches for them. And on one particular occasion I remember feeling very pleased with myself that I'd finished a particular batch of sketches, when a woman came over and had a look at them and rather stonily said, 'Well, they're fine, but there aren't any women in them, there aren't any women's parts.' And I had another look at them and she said, 'Can you do something about this?' And I said, 'Well, yes, I'll see what I can do.' And I went off and sat down and went through it, and it was clearly a quite major task. So what I did in the end was I went through the list of male characters at the side and added an 'a' to the end of any ones that I could, which solved the problem immediately. So, if you come across a bunch of scripts with lots of Ericas and Paulas and Philippas ...

I like to think that if I was dealing with that problem now, I'd deal with it differently, but the fact of the matter is I probably wouldn't have to. Generally speaking, men have always used predominantly male characters in their plays, just as women have used female characters – it's much easier, in terms of familiarity of experience, dialogue, your frame of reference – and as a result, plays of six men and one woman, or two women, five men and one woman who probably takes her top off in Act 2 Scene 3, are quite a constant in British theatre; they're a kind of heavy metal in that they never quite go away.

Having said that, I think I should say that the recent crop of men-only plays would have met with a far frostier reception had it happened at any other period in the last twenty years, particularly the 1980s when there was a greater emphasis on plays about women's experience and a promotion of women writers and female performers. And in fact, if you were a man writing then and you contemplated writing a play without any women, it was quite a serious offence.

So 'trend' is, I suppose, an appropriate word, though it's not quite as flimsy as it might appear; trends tend to suggest something else going on underneath, in a kind of iceberg way. So I think it *is* interesting that there is this group of plays which totally excludes women, and that in spite of that (or perhaps because of it) the success of the plays hasn't been prejudiced. What the exclusivity of the plays suggests to me is that, in contrast with other plays with largely male casts (in which maleness was a inevitable but often incidental by-product), with these plays maleness seems to be very much the main focus of it, that's what they are about, that's what they're looking at. And more, it's a kind of maleness which shows men having some kind of identity crisis – and any insights into their relationship with women have to be gleaned from the relationships between the men themselves, or the men failing to relate to each other. So it's as if a lid is being lifted, or a stone is being turned, and we are given a slightly voyeuristic, warts-and-all view of men in varying group situations, parading both strengths and vulnerabilities, particularly vulnerabilities I think. And this gives the plays for the most part a common thread of self-criticism and self-examination which at the same time roots them very firmly in the 1990s in keeping with other genre writing, whether it's Nick Hornby writing about football or Blake Morrison writing about the death of his father.

Why that should be happening now can be traced back in part to the early 1980s, when radical changes in the employment market meant that men were confronted with the then quite alien prospect of being nurturers instead of breadwinners. It also goes back to 1989 – as so many things in the 1990s do – when a sudden hole was blasted in the middle of so many people's central beliefs, and there was a collective feeling of having the rug pulled from people's feet, which meant that they either lost interest or became pragmatists, or in some cases abandoned their ideals or in other cases chose to channel their energies and frustrations with what was going on around them into single issues: anti-road-building movements, animal liberation, whatever. And the right, seizing that moment and sensing the feeling of confusion in all areas, including sexual politics – certainly heterosexual politics – moved very swiftly, I think, and for example hijacked the whole notion of political correctness by picking on its crazier manifestations and discrediting any early attempts to change the status quo in male–female relationships.

And instead what was offered up, as a token compensation for the harshness of the 1980s and a means of ushering in the caring, sharing 1990s, was the rather flimsy concept of the New Man, which was very much a media concept from the start, targeted very particularly at the middle classes, but which nevertheless a lot of men took on board as something that they might want, and that women might want as well. So they were all the more surprised when actually it went out of fashion and was knocked down, not entirely unfairly, as yet another in a long line of newfangled techniques to get women into bed. Added to which, in its rare genuine manifestations it was dismissed by women as being fundamentally unsexy. And I think that sent confusing messages to men.

So, for those who couldn't hold the baby and shave at the same time – even if they wanted to – the message then seemed to be, well, let's get back to the good old days, when men were men and women were women; and suddenly our television sets were full of *Men Behaving Badly* and quiz games about football, and there were books about football and magazines like *Loaded* and *Maxim* and a whole New Lad syndrome which moved in and seemed to be saying, well, we had a go, it didn't work, boys will be boys, and anyway you love us deep down really, don't you, and we'll look after the kids every second Thursday.

And while I think some of the plays have jumped on that particular bandwagon, I think most haven't, though they've undoubtedly bene-fited from the apparent renewed interest that men's issues enjoy in the media, and in a curious kind of way subverted it for their own needs. What it's allowed the plays to do and the writers to do is to explore a kind of love-hate relationship with what's going on, because there is undeniably something appealing about it, there's a kind of refreshing honesty, in contrast with a certain duplicity that was associated with the New Man era. At the same time, it's not as if it's a leap back to the past days of unthinking sexism ... you clearly can't wipe out forty years of change, however slight.

It would be absurd then for women to feel that they had somehow lost all the ground gained over the last twenty years. After all, it's hard to criticize men for delving into their emotional lives if you've been repeatedly accusing them of not being able to do precisely that. Certainly, if I was a woman writing plays now, I'd be more worried about the return to the six men and two women plays than I would about what was in the end only a passing trend, dealing with genuine contemporary masculine problems.

Mark Ravenhill's first play, *Shopping and Fucking*, was originally produced by Out of Joint and the Royal Court and went on to a West End run, an international tour, and productions in Germany, Holland, Israel, Greece, Scandinavia and New York. His subsequent plays are *Faust is Dead* (Actors Touring Company on tour), the jointly written *Sleeping Around* (Salisbury, Donmar Warehouse and on tour) and most recently *Handbag* (Actors Touring Company), which compares attitudes to sexuality and parenthood at the end of the nineteenth and twentieth centuries.

Kevin Elyot's stage plays include *Coming Clean* (Bush Theatre), an adaptation of *The Moonstone* (Swan Theatre, Worcester), a version of Ostrovky's *Artists and Admirers* (Royal Shakespeare Company), *My Night with Reg*, an award-winning comedy about gay men which transferred from the Royal Court to the Criterion Theatre in 1994, and most recently *The Day I Stood Still* at the National Theatre.

William Gaminara is a writer and an actor, whose plays include an adaptation of Zola's *Germinal* (Paines Plough), *Back Up the Hearse and Let Them Sniff the Flowers* (Hampstead Theatre) and a play about poker, *According to Hoyle*, also at Hampstead, in 1996.

Plays by Women

Clare McIntyre, Winsome Pinnock, Rebecca Prichard

Clare McIntyre

> The younger generation of playwrights with which the British theatre is now richly blessed seem not to be able to work their way out of the studio theatres. I cannot help being disturbed by the fact that none of them have yet provided that kind of rallying point which every theatre-going generation needs to provide a focus for its own wishes and dreams.
>
> David Hare, quoted in the *New Statesman*, 14 March 1997

Women's theatre. What about a gay writer who doesn't write about being gay? Is he a gay writer? What about a woman writer who doesn't write about being of the female sex: is she a woman writer? Categories are a curse. I think there will probably always be fewer female playwrights than male. But twenty years ago there didn't seem to be any of us and now there are lots. That's progress. I think we are judged on our work, but whether you get your play on will depend on who's doing the judging. If women's theatre is supposed to be dead at the moment, it's because of who is doing the judging; that is, who is running the theatres. It's directors who determine what is seen and on what stages.

A list of my particular grievances at the moment is: one, there seems to be an obsession with playwrights being young and new. Second, there isn't the support to enable people to continue once they've started. And that's vital and it has to be there. Three, you have to earn money at it in order to continue. Four, you're not going to do that if you're only put on in small spaces. Five, why do critics tell you what you should be tackling? Six, why do critics lament playwrights going off into telly?

Lastly, there is an assumption that playwrights have opinions on what other playwrights should be writing about and that they have an overview of what the present trend in playwriting is in terms of subject matter, and that they feel a part of that trend. I haven't, I haven't and I don't. I don't write what I do feeling part of a community of writers. I think all writers are individual and are not concerned with what others in their trade are getting up to. I didn't set out to write women's plays, whatever that means. I don't expect *The Thickness of Skin* to appeal more to a female audience than a male. We women writers are at a disadvantage because there are fewer of us and, currently maybe, what we are writing is less appealing. So you change the people making the decisions. Well, they *will* change. The writers will still be here coming up with the work. It's such bloody hard work writing plays, and we're all in such competition with each other trying to work out why the current trend in productions is one thing or another, and that seems to be taking us away from getting on with the work. I mean: it's someone else's debate. Because the one thing I'm bloody sure about is that writers don't have much clout.

What I was trying to do with *The Thickness of Skin* was get the structure of a play right, and doing that meant getting a bigger play. I was effectively moving from writing *Low-level Panic* to writing *The Thickness of Skin*. *Low-level Panic* couldn't actually be longer than an hour and twenty, and structurally it's no bigger than that, whereas *The Thickness of Skin* is. That was my preoccupation.

I think that when someone asks me, 'Have you got a play with a cast of forty up your sleeve – is that something you're dying to do, with huge numbers of people on the stage?' my answer is 'no'. So then I think, 'Am I just domestic, am I just female, am I just introverted about it?' And I don't think that's right either. I think people want to go and see plays in good, smallish theatres where their relationship with the actors is really enjoyable and intimate and close and exciting. They don't actually want to be sitting looking down on a play.

Finally, about writing now, in the 1990s, and there's been quite a lot of reference back to the 1970s at this conference. Well, I was acting in the 1970s, writing now. I didn't want to write about issues, I wanted them to inform my narrative. Had I been writing *The Thickness of Skin* in the 1970s, I'd have written it differently and it would have been the issues: it would have been about homelessness. But, ironically, because *The Thickness of Skin* couldn't be pigeonholed into a play about homelessness, it was hard to knock it. I find that an interesting state of affairs.

Winsome Pinnock

I suppose I feel more ambivalent than Clare does, because initially I was aided by having my work promoted by women within theatres, and by institutions that primarily existed to promote women writers. I'm interested that labelling has become a big subject, because for the writer this becomes very disempowering. And I'm interested in the way in which the label constructs an identity for the writer which excludes a kind of complexity of interpretation. It means that people are unable to move beyond the label to actually see the complex worlds that playwrights are trying to represent.

When I started writing I was constantly being asked whether I considered myself a black playwright, a woman playwright, a black woman playwright or just a playwright – as though I could choose different identities! And about a year ago the *Guardian* ran an article about me and two other women writers, and because we happened to have plays on at the same time, this was construed as a new wave of black women's writing – never mind the fact that one of the writers had written a play in which there were something like six or seven characters, only one of whom was black.

So I don't know how you actually define a writer's identity in that way. And it is very limiting. I don't know what constitutes a woman's play. I wrote a play called *Leave Taking* about ten years ago and I was so fascinated by the history of a community, of people and the way that that history impacts on what is called mainstream culture, and how it redefines one's idea about Englishness. In this play I was preoccupied with the themes of migration and the loss that occurs during migration, the pain of that separation and also the trauma and joy or uneasiness of forging new identities within new locations. And the main characters in that play were a mother and her two daughters; but much as I am fascinated by the relationships in that play and the emotional aspects of it, I don't consider it a mother-daughter play (which is how it's often described). I wrote another play called *Talking in Tongues* which looks at the different sexual and other obsessive relationships within a multi-cultural or multi-racial group of people, and for me that play was again about exploring the changing nature of cultural identities and the collision or clash of cultures; it was about the beginning of something new and the potential for change. And I suppose that was seen as either a play by an angry black woman about inter-racial relationships, or a play about relationships, which again is to reduce what I was trying to make sense of as a playwright.

Whenever my plays have been produced in the Theatre Upstairs, the marketing people have got their so-called black mailing list out, targeting these people. So the audience changes significantly, the theatre is suddenly besieged by a different kind of audience. (And I do wonder why they can't get that list out for other plays as well.) But I like watching audiences: one night they might be all white and the next all black, and yet another night they're mixed. I've had people say to me, 'Oh god, you're writing about me, aren't you?' And these are different kinds of people. The main character is a black cleaner and the women who've told me that she's like them are often completely different.

And when my play *Mules* was on, the first couple of nights were sold out before we'd finished rehearsing, and it was really odd: this play was about young women who traffic drugs – and on the first couple of previews, I'd say the average audience age was about sixty.

But Clean Break theatre company, who commissioned the work, play to two different kinds of audience. *Mules* was written for a prison audience, as the company aims to be the voice of women prisoners and ex-prisoners, and the plays are intended to reflect the experiences of women who've been involved in the criminal justice system. I found it quite complicated in a way, negotiating my own role in creating a play for a prison audience. On the one hand, the brief from Clean Break was to somehow reflect the experiences of those women, but on the other hand I was writing as an outsider and, therefore, as a commentator. So I found that when the play toured prisons, people weren't really saying, 'That's me,' they were saying, 'Yes, I identify with that experience.' And one particular aspect of the play was the joy of transgression, the joy of criminality, and however dangerous that was, we found people identified with it.

I went to another conference recently, entitled 'Reinventing Britain'. It was about cultural hybridity, so that rather than demarcating rigid boundaries between different groups the people there were talking about how the boundaries were being broken down; that ideas about marginality and the minorities are actually shifting. It seems to me that when we look at plays and interpret them, we're not embracing what's actually happening in the world, that there is far more collision and clash and influence between different groups, and that things are breaking down much more than we acknowledge.

Rebecca Prichard

Since I wrote *Essex Girls*, which has an all-woman cast and deals with issues pertinent to women, it might be surprising for me to reject the label of being a maker of women's theatre. But my instinct at the time of writing it was simply that I wanted to work with young people, I wanted to hear real voices, and I found that experience really fed into the energy of the play. But I now think that the audience were allowed to feel very comfortable in their seats. They could watch the play and see the girls in their own world as quite isolated and apart, and either feel liberal enough to empathize with them or not – it was the audience's choice. I'm very proud of my play and I love it, but having had it produced, I am now more aware of my relationship with an audience.

The plays that have most excited me since I wrote *Essex Girls* have been plays where a writer has refused to limit the scope of her work to women's issues, but instead has simply written about the world. I'm thinking in particular of *Blasted* by Sarah Kane or *The Strip* by Phyllis Nagy. I think these plays refuse to see women's insignificance in society as an unfortunate accident which must be corrected by putting women's difficulties, women's experiences, on stage. Instead, they explore a world that is very interconnected; they explore women's insignificance as a symptom of a profoundly abusive power structure in our society which is dehumanizing to both men and women.

I think these kinds of play are much more dangerous, much more potent, as is obvious from the critics' responses to them. In contrast, it seems to me, those plays which are supposed to celebrate masculinity, youth and nihilism, are actually emasculating theatre as a form because they are taking away serious intentions and the playwright's work as a voice of social criticism, and the audience's role as witness, which is one of the few things we have left that makes people feel responsible for others in society. The question has been asked as to why Churchill's *Top Girls* only produced a handful of writers, whereas David Mamet's work has produced a lot. I think it's because everyone keeps saying people are like Mamet, when they're not. In *Glengarry Glen Ross* or *American Buffalo*, I think Mamet explores a world in which the only language left is one of aggression; he explores the link between society's values, society's expectations and brutality – and he never allows the audience to walk away without feeling the human cost of that. In my view, many playwrights who are said to have been influenced by Mamet try to emulate the energy of his dialogue but miss the heart of his work. We end up with plays which are a strange celebration of masculine culture but which at the same time totally emasculate theatre. They are supposed to look at power but they trivialize it. We're supposed to be nihilistic, Generation X youth writers, and that's supposed to be really cool. But I don't feel that. I feel as objectified about being called a young writer as I do about being called a woman writer, simply because when you decide to write and if you are seriously writing then that's what you're doing; it doesn't matter if you're fifteen or fifty-three.

That said, the experience of Clean Break has been interesting. Having just talked about not reflecting women's experience or not wanting to be self-conscious about it, I think it is a difficult concept. I *do* get a lot of strength from working with other women and seeing what issues are particular to women, but I don't think that necessarily prescribes an agenda. There are issues that are pertinent to women but I think they are also pertinent to men.

Clare McIntyre was a member of the Women's Theatre Group from 1978 to 1980. Her plays include *Low-level Panic* (Women's Playhouse Trust), *My Heart's a Suitcase* and *The Thickness of Skin* (both at the Royal Court). She has adapted Stefan Zweig's *Beware of Pity* for the Haymarket Theatre, Leicester.

Winsome Pinnock's stage plays include *Leave Taking* (Liverpool Playhouse, Lyric Hammersmith) and *A Hero's Welcome*, *Talking in Tongues* and *A Rock in Water* (all at the Royal Court). Her play about drug smuggling, *Mules*, was commissioned by Clean Break, a theatre company set up to provide a voice for women prisoners, ex-prisoners and ex-offenders.

Rebecca Prichard's latest play, *Yard Gal*, was presented by Clean Break. Her previous work includes *Essex Girls*, *It Could Be You* and *Fair Game*, a free adaptation of Edna Mazya's *Games in the Backyard* (all for the Royal Court).

Plays on Politics

Andy de la Tour, Cheryl Martin, David Greig

Andy de la Tour

> Andy de la Tour's vengeful, disgracefully enjoyable version of
> New Labour in power, cunningly disguised as an old-fashioned
> drawing-room drama.
> Briefing for *Landslide*, *Independent*, 19 April 1997

Almost all the critics who saw my play *Landslide* talked about the
french windows. Now I'm happy with that, because as every writer
knows, french windows are a fantastically useful way of getting
characters in and out of rooms without having doorbells going and
people saying, 'I wonder who that is?' and having to go out to answer
the door.

But the play has an old-fashioned structure deliberately, because I
hope that within that structure it can say some reasonably funny and
subversive things. It's also an old-fashioned play because it deals with
national politics. The play is about a three-cornered debate between an
old Tory, new Labour and old Labour, which mirrors the debate that's
taking place in the national political scene during the election.

The serious point I want to make is that there is less and less real
political debate in our political life, as we have seen through this
débâcle of an election campaign (which is all about headless chickens
and God knows what else). What we've seen is a growing consensus
that certain things are shared – enterprise good, welfare bad; profit
good, trade unions bad – these concepts are now shared across the
political class. Certain debates about what I think are the real issues in
life are not being had in the real political world, so let's have them in
the theatre.

The other substantial point I wanted to make was that if there is a
hostility to political plays, for want of a better phrase, I don't think it's
because the audiences are hostile to those plays; I think the audiences

on the contrary are extremely interested in plays which deal with the crisis in our institutions, that deal with international politics, that deal with the media as a whole. I suspect that some of the hostility to political drama, to overtly political drama, is coming from the theatre establishment. And despite some honourable exceptions, like David Hare's trilogy at the National, I wonder if there isn't too narrow a cultural agenda being set by theatre managements themselves.

I'm not talking now about the commercial sector. I don't expect Bill Kenwright to put on a play about the crisis in the education system. But I think that there's a danger that the subsidized London theatres are setting too narrow a trend and perhaps following fashions that they should be consciously and deliberately resisting.

I'll finish with a quote from a survey that was done about attitudes amongst adolescents, where they asked a thousand young people in Northumberland, Sussex and Birmingham about their lives and their attitudes. The results were very interesting. Seventy per cent had signed petitions on issues such as human rights; nearly 60 per cent had boycotted goods; 48 per cent had campaigned on local issues such as loss of greenfield sites or transport closures. Are our theatre managements and artistic directors doing enough to get young writers to write about those things, and to widen from their own personal experience to the issues that affect us all?

Cheryl Martin

I've just done a play with the Birmingham-based Banner Theatre, who are definitely rooted in the 1970s agitprop tradition; they write folk songs and they're very up-front and very definitely political. A friend of mine who saw *Redemption Song* described it as an all-singing, all-dancing pamphlet, and I think that is a fair description.

But I want to explain why I did this particular play, and why I'll stick up for it. It's partly because, for a lot of people, there's a choice about whether they're political or not. They feel they can be apolitical or another day they can be political.

I remember when I was about six or seven years old, in a playground back in the States, having some Italian girl telling me to get back to Africa, and by the time I was six I knew enough to tell her that I was part Cherokee, I belonged here and she could go back to Europe. So, if you have already been politicized by the time you're six years old from people calling you nigger, it's not something that you've chosen exactly. I was living in Salford during the Iran–Iraq war, and my husband, who's blond and blue-eyed, was down in the pub waiting for me. And although it was a really rough pub, we didn't usually have any trouble; but this time, as soon as I walked in the door it's the NF in the corner, and it's 'bomb all the Pakis, bomb all the Yids, bomb all the niggers and all their kids'. And I think that that's why a lot of my plays tend to be political.

However, I have to say that the Banner play is atypical of most of my plays. Usually I try to smuggle the politics in; you write a cracking family drama and you get the politics embedded in the story. Banner's style is very up-front, very in-your-face, and when I first started writing with them we fought for a year about exactly how we were going to do the play, because I don't like folk music and I wanted to be a bit more oblique and I wanted to bring the poetry in, and I didn't want to hector the audience, I wanted to drag them in with an emotional through-line. Whereas *they* wanted a lot of different political points made: for instance, it had to have a trade-union element, it had to be up-beat at the end. (At this point I thought they'd never read anything I wrote – mine usually end with an assassination or murder or somebody going insane.)

The play ended up being about asylum seekers, and especially about the detention centre where the woman that I based the main character on went through a hunger strike and nearly died. And since they wanted a trade-union element, I wanted to concentrate on one of the guards, and say, 'This is a working-class woman, let's look at why she thinks it's OK to treat people this way, let's look at what brought her to this point.' But what I got back from the company was, 'Oh no, you can't talk about them. Why are you going to spend resources talking about people like that?' They felt their audience would not be interested in this person, that they would be totally alienated by it. So I said, 'OK, all right'.

I think that parts of the final product are more successful than others. But this is the only one of my plays where people have actually come up to me on the street and said, 'I really love that play. I am so glad you talked about that.' When you're doing community plays, you start off with people's lives and you get that buzz, a feeling that you're telling a story that wouldn't normally get told. But this is the only one where black people have actually been stopping me in the street and saying, 'You know, that really meant something to me.' Not to mention that there are asylum seekers in the cast, and a lot of deportation campaigns consider this part of their political work. So it *is* an all-singing, all-dancing pamphlet and that's the way it's being used. It wasn't meant to go to the Bush Theatre; it's not for that audience at all.

So I think that it definitely has a place. And even though I'm very ambivalent about it because it's not what I would normally go to myself, I still think it's valid to have done it, because Banner has a long tradition, and a very loyal audience, and it's talking about stuff nobody else will talk about.

And when you consider the general election campaign, most people are completely missing from any of these issues. Black people are totally missing, the politicians don't give a shit whether we vote for them or not; what difference does it make what we do? We can kill ourselves – they don't care. So you do feel you have to communicate some of that frustration.

As a poet, when I want to write something purely personal, I do it through poetry, and that audience is a different audience – it's usually white and middle-class, whether you're a black poet or not. And you do that in a different language, you do it through your dense, dazzling imagery or whatever; then it's a different language, a different audience, a different reason.

A lot of the other black writers I know in Manchester don't even consider theatre any more. They might have done some theatre before, but people go 'Eeegh!' when you talk about the way that things are marketed. You get a feeling sometimes that, as a black writer, they cannot market you. At least the Royal Court Theatre Upstairs has *got* a black mailing list.

But I think that things could change if you could show people a little chink of light. I think that what goes on with a lot of people I see is despair. When you go through year after year after year, wishing that things could be better, you see nobody working, you see people who were working now doing part-time jobs, you see that you're not going to have social security when you get old, you're going to be living on cat food. That may not be true for people who are living in Hampstead Heath, but it's true for a lot of people who are living in Salford Precinct or in Moss Side.

What happens in despair is that you lapse into silence. If you stop communicating, then there is no possibility of healing whatever wounds people are feeling. And I see some of my friends slipping into silence, as far as theatre is concerned.

David Greig

The question I am most interested in asking is whether the very idea of writing about politics might in some way be prehistoric. In my experience of the theatre, it is considered slightly embarrassing now to take yourself, your work or the work of other people seriously on a fundamental political level, but also to a certain extent on an artistic level. And I think this has coincided with the idea that there is perhaps a golden age or a new writing boom or that audiences are coming back to the theatre. In a general cultural context, it's a little bit like all the other arts welcoming theatre at last into the bar and saying, 'Oh terrific, you're not going to hector us any more and you're not going to bring up those tiresome issues that you always do: you're actually going to talk about babes or you're going to tell us some weird urban myths. And that will be much more entertaining for everybody.'

I don't personally buy into that. I do take what I do seriously politically. The main reasons for this are twofold. One is a personal interest in belief and all questions about belief which I find central to my own way of thinking about the world and the way that I observe other people thinking about the world. And the second reason is to do with the very practice of theatre itself and the politics inherent in that.

For the purposes of this debate, I would like to draw a distinction between writing about politics and political theatre. I think it's possible for writing about politics not to be political and I think it's possible for writing that is not about politics to be intensely political. What I would call political theatre makes interventions into ideology. It deals into ideology. It poses questions about society to which it does not already know the answer. And perhaps most importantly, political theatre has at its very heart the possibility of change.

If you look at the 1990s, there is no choice in the election campaign. There is no possibility of change. There is a possibility of a change of administration but no serious engagement with the idea of change – to

66

the extent that, when faced with corruption, the response of our party political system is to put up a man in a white suit, a journalist, as a paragon of virtue, as an anti-corruption candidate. Now I'm sure he is a very virtuous man. But the abdication of responsibility in that gesture was so breathtaking, and so uncommented upon, that it amazed me.

I think there are other elements to which we can look in the political culture. Interestingly, in Scotland the Nationalists are retreating from nationalism, in the sense that they propose independence but they're almost embarrassed about the idea that they may have an ideology. I wouldn't necessarily support their ideology if they did, but I think it's interesting that all the parties, even the Nationalists (who have the most practical change to offer if they could get everyone to vote for them) are retreating from ideology. There is a sense that ideology itself is embarrassing, that no one believes that things can ever change or ought ever to be changed in the political culture. I think this comes out of the collapse of the left but also the collapse of the right. Thatcher as an ideologue burned the hands of many right-wing people about the very concept of an ideology and about changing society. And if you look further back, a period of great interest to me is the 1930s when ideology was the heart of every single thing. Ordinary working-class people were constantly dealing in battles of ideology, so much so that they physically fought them out on the street. If you look at the events of the 1940s and then the discoveries of the 1950s about those events in Russia and in Germany, I think that also signals partly why we may have retreated from ideology.

Even the non-political culture is based on stasis. If we look at the Swampies of this world, Green politics, Internet politics, they too sell themselves on their own lack of ideology. So greenness is seen as being a non-ideological position and therefore one where, famously, the grannies in Kent could protest against animal exports and so could the young punk rocker. There is a sense in which everyone is assumed to agree about these things, which finally finds its apotheosis artistically in the figure of Renton, the junkie in *Trainspotting*, who has become the lifestyle icon of our times.

I'm sure everybody is familiar with the various ways this manifests itself in the culture. Whatever the qualities of the piece of art in and of itself, it seems to me that stasis is at the very heart of the portrayals of junkiedom, and particularly the drug heroin. They're about stillness, they're about falling asleep, as far as I can make out – about coma. Speed was the drug of choice in the early 1980s. There's a profound difference between the effect that speed has on political culture and the effect that heroin does.

Within this culture of stasis, then, we come to political theatre. I've already said I believe that the possibility of change has to be at the heart of theatre which I would call political. However entertaining and interesting it may be simply to take a snapshot of a group of people in a particular place at a particular time living out their lives, in the way that a film like *Trainspotting* did, it's ultimately of no use.

The other element of this possibility of change is that it doesn't necessarily have to be change in terms of 'then socialism happens' at the end of a play; it's change on every level. It's admitting the possibility of fantasy. It's admitting the possibility of the individual changing the individual circumstances, the individual's desires changing. It's also admitting the possibility – and this is something I'm profoundly interested in – that the person's beliefs may change. A running theme in my work is a fascination with people who believe things that they know not to be true: people who are able to retain faith in problematic ideologies, whether they be socialism, communism or Christianity. It's within these areas that I think plays have to deal. Now that may take place in a party political context, but it's just as likely that it will take place in a prison cell or in a supermarket. These debates and these images and these possibilities can be raised.

I'd like to look at the political act of theatre itself. Everyone will be familiar with the fact that theatres are often the first places to be closed at times of political crisis, because they are places where people gather together, and that in itself is profoundly political. Perhaps it doesn't seem that way in Britain just now, but in many parts of the world the very act of gathering is a political act, and this has been so throughout history. The second element is that the foundation of theatre as an art form is based in religion. I'm not a Christian, but I think that the religious aspect of theatre, the coming together of people, actual human beings in organic proximity to each other, is what makes it a place where politics should be discussed. Television is very good at raising things and has other jobs it can do, but a play has to carry along the people in the room, because ultimately they can shout out, 'This is fucking rubbish,' if they want to. You can shout at the television, and people do, but it makes no difference to the art continuing. The communality of theatre, and its foundation in a kind of spiritual ritual of transformation, is to me what makes it the most important place in which these questions of change, these questions of belief, can be discussed by society.

So, lastly I'd like to come to my work. I have worked most often in 300-seat theatres in Scotland. To sell 300 seats in Edinburgh is very different from selling 300 seats in London. You're not talking to an élite group if you sell 300 seats in Edinburgh. Selling sixty seats in a city of ten million is very different to selling 300 seats in a city of half a million. The people who came to my plays did not expect swearing and many of them winced when they heard it. Some of them were regular theatregoers, but some had never seen plays before. There was a cross-section in that audience and they were coming to see a play set in their city – ostensibly – by a writer who lives amongst them. And that in itself was very powerful and one of the reasons why the play sold. So I would dispute this idea that political work doesn't sell. In fact, the experience of the Traverse would be that it's non-political work that doesn't sell, that doesn't create debate or bring audiences in.

Andy de la Tour's prophetic play about a Labour *Landslide* was performed during the 1997 election campaign at West Yorkshire Playhouse and the Birmingham Repertory Theatre. His other stage plays include *Viva!* (Theatre Royal, Stratford East), *Here We Go* (Crucible, Sheffield), *Safe in Our Hands* and an adaptation of Dario Fo's *The Pope and the Witch* (both West Yorkshire Playhouse).

Cheryl Martin was born in Washington DC and is a poet, singer and songwriter as well as a playwright. Her stage work includes *Dhalta Suraj* (with the Bolton Asian community for Pit Prop Theatre) and *Heart and Soul* (the Oldham Coliseum Theatre community play). In 1995 she collaborated with Birmingham's socialist theatre group Banner Theatre on *Redemption Song*; since then she has written the community play *Avalanche* for Nottingham Playhouse, where she was associate artist. She is developing *Phillis* for Notttingham (based on the life of the eighteenth-century poet Phillis Wheatley, the first black poet to be published).

David Greig's plays include *Petra's Explanation* (Traverse Theatre, Edinburgh), *Stalinland* (Edinburgh Fringe and Citizens' Theatre, Glasgow), *Europe*, *One Way Street*, *The Architect* (all at the Traverse) and the collaborative work *Timeless* (Donmar Warehouse and tour).

About Then: History Plays

Diane Samuels, Timberlake Wertenbaker, April de Angelis

Diane Samuels

> It may still be decades or even centuries before humankind stops regarding the knowledge stored up in the unconscious as immaterial, as pathological fantasies of the insane, or eccentric poets, and comes to see it for what it really is, a perception of reality, stemming from the period of early childhood, which had to be relegated to the unconscious, where it becomes an inexhaustible source of artistic creativity, of the imagination *per se*, of fairy tales and dreams ... Once such knowledge is legitimised as pure imagination, all doors are open to it.
>
> Alice Miller, *Thou Shalt Not Be Aware* (Pluto, 1984)

I'd like to start with a story. It's a true story and it's about history. It's set in Liverpool, in the Jewish community where I grew up. In this community – which was more like a ghetto than you might expect in 1970s Britain, made up of immigrants who had come over from Eastern Europe mostly at the end of the nineteenth, beginning of the twentieth century, and their descendants – was a school. I went to that school. It was a Jewish school. We were taught Hebrew and Jewish Studies, which included Jewish history. When we were about fourteen the time came for us to learn something from our heritage which was very important. We were taken into a room and the television was turned on. There was no preparation. We hadn't talked about what was going to happen to us. We were shown a film which lasted about an hour, about the concentration camps. We weren't expecting it and were very shocked by it. At the end, the Head of Jewish Studies, an orthodox rabbi, closed the door and said to us, 'That is why we have to have the state of Israel.' That is history turned into propaganda.

And I believed what he said for a number of years, because the shock of seeing the film and the message I was given afterwards profoundly affected me. How does one survive that? How does one live after such a thing? And I thought, 'Well, you have to have the state of Israel. This is what I have been told.' This was strangely confirmed by my study of mainstream history. The Holocaust was mentioned, but mostly the experience of the Second World War wasn't focused around it. It tended to be given a paragraph or two. Now I found that very strange. Here I was, being told that this was the major event in twentieth-century history, and here it was a footnote. That partly confirmed my feeling that we had to have the state of Israel, because if no one was going to recognize that experience, then that was the answer.

Then, when I was a little older I started to meet young people who had visited the Occupied Territories. I started to meet Palestinian students and they told me, 'These are the things that are happening to us and this is why we need the state of Palestine.' And so I started to ask questions.

What began to interest me is the way history is appropriated and used for political means in the present. If we don't know about the history then we are victims of the political propaganda. And the more we know about the history, the less we are its victims.

I just wonder about how much we live without knowing what happened to us; not only in our own personal lives, but in the collective lives of our cultures and our societies. What fascinates me is that there is recorded and remembered history, and then there is the unrecorded and untold and unremembered history. Where is it? I don't think it's gone. I don't believe that, just because we don't consciously remember something, we lose it. Hearing young men today talk about their sense of dislocation, I'm struck by the thought that there was a holocaust for this country in the twentieth century that isn't entirely owned.

I grew up with the Holocaust-this, the Holocaust-that, Jewish experience-this, 'you must remember', etc. At the beginning of this century, millions of British men were slaughtered in Europe. And I don't know what your grandfathers and great-grandfathers did, but what did they tell you about it? Where have you been told this recorded experience? What do you know? That's hidden. You've got it. Maybe some of the anxiety and the pain now comes from what happened then that's never been dealt with. A whole generation of young British men were murdered by their fathers. I think that's an astonishing thing. Why isn't it talked about? Where does it go?

It goes into other places: into physical infirmities perhaps, into anxieties we don't know the cause of, into our dreams, the way we treat our children, the way we treat 'others'. It goes into our fantasies, into pornography, into everything – all these unspoken ways that are part of the texture and implicit fabric of our lives. Part of this unconscious heritage is connected to a culture of denial. And denial doesn't eradicate: quite the opposite. It simply forces other modes of expression. It's this territory that absolutely fascinates me.

Timberlake Wertenbaker

When David invited me to this conference, he said, 'Oh well, you know about the past, why don't you talk about the past?' I thought, 'OK, the eighteenth century, maybe the Greeks'. I didn't realize that the distant, forgotten, silent past would be the 1980s. But I will go to the past, and I am going to go straight to Greece because, while we may not agree about John Osborne, we may not agree about the 1990s, we can all agree there was actually a golden age of theatre and it was fifth-century Athens, and it had Aeschylus, Sophocles and Euripides as well as Aristophanes, and they spanned not three months but a whole century. Sophocles wrote his last play at the age of ninety. (In an age when the average shelf-life of a playwright is three months, I would love to think that some of us might still be writing at ninety.) This period spanned a hundred years and it was extremely varied. If you look at the plays that we have left (and they are very few), you get a fantastic variety. You get the imaginative, religious, earthbound; you get rationalism, you get the no-plot-but-good-dialogue syndrome; the two plots in one play problem. It's all there.

Some fifty years after this fantastic age, along came Aristotle and proceeded to take this rich landscape and reduce it to one playwright, and indeed one play of one playwright. I'm paraphrasing Aristotle quite broadly, but it's true: he said there's only one good play and that's *Oedipus Rex* and that's because it has one character, one action, it takes place over a short span of time and it's all in one place. It's contained. He also said some interesting things about pity and terror, but basically he reduced this to one kind of play. And I think that the *Poetics* wrecked theatre for the next two thousand years. Of course I'm exaggerating, but there are very few good plays by the Romans and it's not just because they were building lavatories. It's because they had all read Aristotle and it had a deadening impact. And I think that what we are getting now is the proliferation of Aristotles, and the reduction of playwriting. And I think this is the problem of the 1990s.

The Elizabethans freed themselves from those constraints of time and place that suited Racine and strangled others. What we have now in Britain is some people trying to reduce what has been, over the century, a rich landscape. Most of us at this conference have only mentioned the last five years or the last two years. There is always an attempt to reduce it, to say, 'This is what a play looks like: this is what a contemporary play looks like. This is what a play should be. It has to be this. If it's not this, it's not contemporary; if it's not that, it's passé. If it's not written by somebody who looks like this' – and we've come to that – 'it's not a good play, it's not an interesting play.' I think this is a terrible danger and we should be very, very wary of it. And I think playwrights should protest and critics should protest, because the people who are making these cultural judgements are not playwrights; they're not even critics. They're people who say proudly on the front pages of their magazines, 'I don't go to the theatre, but this is what I think about contemporary theatre.' You get endless comments like this: 'I don't go, but I know and I heard and this is what it's like.' And just as we no longer have people reporting from foreign places because it's too expensive for newspapers to actually send reporters out, pretty soon I think critics will be told not to bother to go to the theatre but actually just to write about the theatre in general because it's cheaper and you don't even have to pay for the taxi.

A word that has not been mentioned is humanism. It seems to me that we've talked a little bit about identity, how you recognize yourself and who recognizes what in a play, and how satisfying it is for the playwright to hear someone say, 'That's me'; and how this seems to be happening less and less – or rather, people are more and more specific about what they are willing to recognize as 'me'. And whether it's a failure of the playwright or whether it's a failure of the audience, or whether it is simply something that is happening in fashion, I think it is very serious that no one now goes to a play and looks at a man or a woman, or an old man or a young woman, and says, 'That's me.' The idea now is that you look for your externals, so that you see a young gay male and you say, 'That's me.' But you look at King Lear and you don't say, 'That's me.' Well, I see King Lear and I think, 'Well, that's me – that's as much me as anything else.'

I don't want to talk a lot about women's playwriting because I don't like this compound term, but I wonder if part of the problem is that audiences haven't yet been trained to see a contemporary woman on a stage and actually identify with her. And that is possibly why a lot of women do go into the past when they write characters, because you can at least avoid the immediate alienation of an audience saying, 'Well, this is a woman dressed like that and she's a young woman. She's living in the twentieth century – that's not me. I'm male, I'm young, I'm old, or whatever.' There is some kind of dislocation in us, and I think it's worrying that we don't want to identify with the humanity of someone else any more. If you say, 'Does character still exist?' I think you're saying, 'Does the human being still exist at the end of this century?' I hope the human being can be retrieved from the 'fashionability', from the Aristotles and the Aristotalitarianism of the world. It is not only the history of the twentieth century that is in danger of being wiped out. There's a whole cultural history that is constantly in danger of being wiped out by the Aristotles, who say, 'There weren't really a lot of plays in fifth-century Athens, there was one.'

Unfortunately, the cultural history that has been consistently wiped out over the centuries and is once again under threat of erasure is women's writing. The Aristotles of our age are rewriting history. When lazy commentators say there was no theatre in the 1980s, they mean there was very little male theatre. In fact, the 1980s saw an explosion of writing from women, first in small theatres, often in all-women companies, and later on the bigger stages. This writing was often blatantly feminist and by definition made men uncomfortable. Sarah Daniels's blisteringly funny first play at the Royal Court caused as much discomfort as Sarah Kane's, although the discomfort was expressed more subtly by the male critics. Like feminism itself, women's plays moved into more humanistic, complex concerns and reached an increasingly wide audience. Some time in the late 1980s the Royal Court discovered that it had inadvertently programmed an all-women season. For the first time, women might have begun to feel safe in their work, but that was not counting the backlash that was soon to follow – so that when in the 1990s Stephen Daldry staged his Royal Court Classics season, not only were all the plays by men, but out of thirty characters on stage, only one was a woman, or rather a young girl. I don't think any of this is a conscious male plot – indeed, I doubt it's even an unconscious one – it is simply that writing by women has never fitted neatly into Aristotelian definitions, the dictatorship of current convention, and rather than deal with its complexities, commentators prefer to ignore it.

We've talked a lot about the 'dumbing down' of culture, which is an American word; and of course 'dumbing down' in America means becoming stupid. In English it means 'becoming silent'. So when you use it in the American sense, it has a kind of 'cuteness' and it's rather fun. We're getting stupider, but it's not really stupid. It's OK to be stupid, that's part of contemporary culture. If you translate this into English, we could say that we're also being silenced; that actually the 'dumbing down' of culture, possibly by television or by the media, or even by ourselves, is a gradual silencing. Perhaps this is something more worrying than we'd like to admit.

The other phrase that has come in from America is 'emotional intelligence'; a very fashionable phrase. It seems to me that the history of playwriting is probably the struggle of 'emotional intelligence' against the 'dumbing down' of whoever felt like 'dumbing down' the society at the time. Emotional intelligence is defined in various ways, but it is essentially the ability to make links, the ability to find the relationships, and I think that is what theatre is about: it is the ability to make links between people, between past and present, to draw out, to come to a truth, to come to a revelation about something. We as playwrights also make links, and we ought to encourage our emotional intelligence. And I think that any playwright who comes up and says, 'I have no links,' or 'My link covers a great void,' is actually dumbing himself or herself down.

The world may be fragmented. I don't think playwrights are fragmented. I think we are all linked. I think we can all learn quite a lot from each other if we bother to see each other's plays and if we're encouraged to read each other's plays. I urge us all, and also urge the commentators, the Aristotles, to resist 'dumbing down', to encourage emotional intelligence and find our links.

April de Angelis

I want to start off by talking about form. Every dramatic form comes out of a historical period, what Raymond Williams used to call a structure of feeling. So that things like naturalism, men being trapped in rooms but created by other men, has been with us for a long time, even if it's been bent and changed. And at the heart of that form is an idea about who we are. We are people who have a history, who have depth, who have an inside, and a lot of the way in which plays traditionally worked is that that inside has to be drawn or driven out of us by circumstances, and it is a conflict between the inside and the outside that gives us conflict and depth. And that's how we think of ourselves, that there's a structure of feeling, the way we operate in the world and who we are. And that's not necessarily conservative or radical. But as the world changes, the form will change and then it will no longer be relevant.

We all recognize an intoxication with what's going to happen next, and the way it disappears what's happened before. If you believe we're the post-modern age (as opposed to the modern age, which created those men in rooms struggling against the environment and having their insides denied to them); if we are to think about the world now (as opposed to the world of one hundred years ago, which created the kind of way we look at the world and the kind of way we write characters), I wonder if we're still entitled to write the kind of characters that have an inside that struggles with the outside and where eventually this struggle brings out some kind of truth.

When I start thinking about plays, I suppose I always accept that notion of character, but there's always a part of me that doesn't really believe it. I really want to believe we have a history, I want to believe we have an inside that's us and that will eventually come out, a truth that is the sum of us and what's happened to us in our histories that will emerge and reveal who we are. But even as I write it, I don't believe it.

I don't think problems are a bad thing to have – that's how new forms are made. You think, 'Well, I could write like this and I will write this person and this happened to them ten years ago and now they meet someone and there's a clash and, great, that's drama.' But it doesn't sit easily on me. It's almost like a denial of the world we're in now; I'm not sure that the world that created those forms is here any

77

more. But nor do I want to have people wandering around called A and B, bouncing off each other – I think that's tedious and boring. So it remains a problem.

This was really brought home to me when I saw Martin Crimp's *Attempts on Her Life* upstairs at the Royal Court. I went there and sat and watched and I felt this incredible sense of relief. I thought, 'Thank God, there aren't any people in this play!' It felt so incredibly refreshing. But it also felt really terrifying: if they aren't people, then what on earth are they, and who are we? This play did not define the idea of character: it says we can no longer claim to engage with an art form that lies to us and tells us these kind of people exist, and therefore also says to us, 'You are not who you think you are, you are enjoying an art form you are not really entitled to.' At one point one of the voices in the play believes she's a TV screen, that everything from the front looks real and alive but round the back there's just a few wires. And the playwright believes that we're now in a non-human age, an age of globalization, a new multinational capital, an age of surface depthlessness – we're living in an advert. And at one point there isn't a character on stage, there's a car, the person on stage is a car, and the celebration of the aerodynamic, the body of the car, the way it moves through a space, a beautiful exotic landscape; but there's no people in this landscape, the people are deliberately excluded from it, we don't want then complicating our scenic backdrop. And I was thinking about the Ogoni people and about when they struggled with Shell, the multinational company that has its tentacles everywhere, all that happened was the Ogoni leaders were murdered and the logo of Shell continued to shine out brightly over our world – and nothing happened.

Perhaps the story of the Ogoni has a further resonance for us. Their land is being ecologically destroyed by a global corporation whose god is profit. Should we, like them, be asking how much history we have left?

Diane Samuels' award-winning 1992 play *Kindertransport* concerns Jewish children evacuated from Germany before the war, and was produced by the Soho Theatre Company, the Palace Theatre Watford and in the West End; her other theatre work includes plays for young people produced at the Unicorn Theatre, Theatre Centre, SNAP People's Theatre Trust and Quicksilver Theatre Company, whose production of her Children's Crusade play, *One Hundred Million Footsteps*, was toured in 1997.

Timberlake Wertenbaker's historical plays include *The Grace of Mary Traverse* (Royal Court), the award-winning *Our Country's Good* (Royal Court, then Garrick Theatre) and *After Darwin* (Hampstead, 1998); her other plays include *The Love of the Nightingale* (based on the Philomele myth, RSC), *Three Birds Alighting on a Field* (Royal Court) and *The Break of Day* (Out of Joint tour). She translated the Theban Plays for the RSC.

April de Angelis's history plays include *Ironmistress* (ReSisters Theatre Company), an adaptation of *The Life and Times of Fanny Hill* (Red Shift) and *Playhouse Creatures* (Sphinx, revived at the Old Vic); her contemporary plays are *Hush* (Royal Court) and *The Positive Hour* (Out of Joint tour). Her new play for the Royal Shakespeare Company, *A Warwickshire Testimony*, opens at the Other Place, Stratford, in August 1999.

About Us: Family Plays

Christopher Hampton, Peter Whelan, Sebastian Barry, John Mortimer

Christopher Hampton

> There's no reason you should ever have heard of me. I had a
> certain reputation about ten years ago. You know, in the theatre.
> In Germany. I was considered – you know that word, when they
> don't really like you but think you might not go away –
> promising. I had a play in rehearsal when the Nazis came in. It
> never opened. After that, no one would put on my plays in
> Germany, however bad I tried to make them.
> Odön von Horvath, 1901–38 (in real life) and 1901–51 (in *Tales from
> Hollywood*)

When I first started writing I noticed that several of the writers I most
admired evidently wrote from their own lives. I'm thinking in
particular of John Osborne and David Mercer, whom I got to know
somewhat, who took elements of their own lives and wrestled them
into some sort of dramatic form.

Now there seemed to me that there were some problems with this
approach. One was an objective problem, which was that the trouble
with feeding on your own life was that it somehow came out with
greatest energy the first time and then tended to be repetitious and to
come forth with diminishing energy. And the other was subjective: that
of course you were obliged to lead these exhausting lives and throw
yourself from one terrifying event to another, as David certainly did –
falling off trains and picking up cellists in Hamburg and whatever.
And you could see if you knew him a bit that his whole life was a
process of living these events and then anecdotally polishing them as
he spoke to you, so that you could see that the fact that somebody his
brother once knew had been on the first nuclear submarine which went
under the North Pole was slowly transmuted by David over the course
of months into an absolute conviction that *he* was on the submarine

that went under the North Pole. He was then somehow able to imagine going under the North Pole a great deal more vividly, no doubt, than the person who actually had gone under the North Pole, who probably found it a deeply boring experience.

And so subjectively I decided that this was really not a route that I could follow because, apart from not having the constitution or the stamina for it, I just hadn't had the life experience and was actually unlikely to, given the gruelling nature of the life you had to lead to produce interesting enough drama.

So the only way that I'd written autobiographically to start with was in a sort of oblique and indirect way. The second play I wrote was called *Total Eclipse*, which was about the poets Rimbaud and Verlaine, and while it stayed as close as possible to the actual facts that we know about them, the play also served a sort of therapeutic purpose for me in that it investigated what was involved in being a writer, what were the responsibilities of a writer. So that dealing with two completely different kinds of writers who were also lovers, you were able to think about whether you wanted to be the kind of writer who went pell-mell for experience and burned yourself out, as Rimbaud did, or whether you wished to be a more professional figure who would take it more slowly and decline into a drunken and complacent old age, as Verlaine did. So the biographical element was to examine those questions.

Later on I wrote a play called *Tales from Hollywood*, which is about the German writers in Hollywood during the war, and I was able to smuggle a little autobiography into that because I had a semi-imaginary central character (Odon von Horvath, who actually died in an accident in Paris in 1938), to whom I was able to give some of my experiences, such as the American company that commissioned me to write a film about Edward II and was scandalized to receive a script in which the king of England was a homosexual. Or the end of the play, which mirrored my very first experience in Hollywood, which was that I nearly killed myself in somebody's swimming pool, cutting my head open when there was no one else there; I could easily have drowned in the pool. So instead of taking this as a warning about Hollywood, I took no notice of it in practical terms but simply put it into my play later on.

So I'm really speaking as somebody who had an aversion to writing autobiographical plays until – and this is often the way things happen – Richard Eyre came up with a brilliant plan, which was he would ask David Hare to write a play about Hungary and at the same time (because he knew that I'd been in Egypt in 1956) he would ask me to write a play about Suez. So that's how the project began that became *White Chameleon*. What happened was that David thought a great deal about Hungary and decided that he was more interested in writing a trilogy about British institutions and so went to Richard and said, 'I don't want to write a play about Hungary, I want to write a play about British institutions.' Whereas the more research I did, the less interested I became in writing about a play about the Suez crisis in the terms we'd originally discussed and the more I fell to thinking that this childhood that I'd had between the years of 1952 and 1956 in Egypt had somehow turned me into the person that I became. And when I said to Richard that I was getting more and more like an old man in his dotage sitting there dreaming about the past, he very sportingly said, 'All right, don't write about Suez, write about that.' And so that's how it came about.

There's one other observation I'd like to make which is perhaps of some interest, which is a strange thing. Whenever I'd written bio-graphical pieces – about Verlaine and Rimbaud, about the German writers in Hollywood, about Brecht and Thomas Mann, about Carrington and Lytton Strachey – it had been for some reason an obsession of mine not to make anything up. I was proceeding from the opinion that what actually happens is far stranger and far more interesting than what I could invent, and whenever I've tackled a biographical subject I've found that to be the case; in other words, I've always found that what really happened, however difficult it is to connect the dots (as it were), however illogically people behave, nevertheless what they do is more interesting when you are dealing with real people than what you might imagine they do. On the other hand, writing about myself I felt perfectly free to make up whatever I felt like. So that my autobiographical pieces are a great deal less reliable than my biographical pieces.

Peter Whelan

Let me go into the darker regions of using members of one's family as a basis for creating characters in plays. I have a brother: he's four years older than me; he's very different from me, very tall, powerfully built;

a shock of dark hair when he was young, while I was fair. He always had a quality about him that I felt I would never possess. Right from a very early age (before I could even hope to define it), he was more at ease with the world than I was and seemed to be able to control his situation in it much better than I.

When he was thirteen and I was nine (this was during the war years), our family home was a bungalow on the outskirts of Stoke-on-Trent. We shared a bedroom, and when our parents ordered us to put out the light, we still carried on whispering, talking across the gap between the beds. (At that time we didn't have any great expectation when we went to bed of not having to get up again and go down to the shelter when the Germans came over in an hour's time.) He decided to regularize this and announced that he'd had this idea that we should tell each other stories: that he would tell a story one night and I would tell a story to him the next. That was the way he put it to me, and I was astonished and delighted. I can remember thinking that what I wanted to do most in the world was to tell stories and here my brother, no less, had opened the gates to it.

He told the first story – I don't think I listened to it properly, because whirling round in my mind was what I was going to tell the next night. I do remember thinking his story wasn't all that good, and I thought that, despite the fact that he had this indefinable quality that I shall never have, I felt (even at the age of nine) I'd got the edge on him in telling stories. So the next night I started to tell my story and it was full of wonderful flights of fancy, but he stopped me before I was very far into it. 'This isn't the idea,' he said. 'You're making that up out of your head. That's cheating. You must tell me something that actually happened.'

I was terribly shocked by this; I had to scrabble about and think what had happened during the day, and nothing much seemed to have done. I started to embellish it, but he could always tell. 'You're cheating, I can tell by the tone of your voice.' This was in the dark in the bedroom, all very traumatic.

Well, I went on to be a playwright and he, would you believe, went on to become an inspector of police. And no doubt, when petty criminals came in front of him, as inspector of police of Burslem he'd say, 'You're cheating! You made that up.'

And I've spent my writing life caught between that cheating, childish attitude of wanting to make up stories and the shadow of this police inspector falling across me saying, 'Stick to the facts.'

Why am I nervous about facts? I mean, I *can* work with facts, I've done drama documentary and I've worked with *boxes* of facts. Why am I made nervous about it? I can't nail it on my brother. I've made shamelessly free with members of the family in my play. I've used bits of my sister, my mother, my father, two of my aunts (or is it three?), my wife, one uncle, my father-in-law, my mother-in-law (twice!) and on one occasion even the family dog, though that was just in a reminiscence on stage and besides the animal was dead.

But there is one escape hatch that I've used – twice – and that is to base a character on a member of my family that I've never met. They're usually people who are legendary in the family, that the others talk about a lot (essential, because you're going to have to piece them together from what is said about them). I did it in a play called *The Accrington Pals* and I did it twice in *The Bright and Bold Design*. In *The Accrington Pals* the central character is a woman who runs a greengrocery stall in Accrington during the First World War, and she's a very businesslike woman who doesn't bring much comfort to the people around her. She was based on an aunt that I never met, who disappeared from Salford in 1912. The aunt worked for the Chilprufe Underwear Corporation as a seamstress and they obviously valued her because they took her down to London when the firm moved from Manchester. But apart from a couple of postcards, we never heard of her again. Then in the 1950s my father rang me and said the police had contacted him from London and said that she'd died alone in an attic flat in Paddington and he'd been traced as the only next of kin – having not heard from her in forty years.

So I went along with him to see where she'd lived and it was a dreadful flat. It was smelly, it was cold. Snow was actually coming in through a broken pane. She hadn't looked after herself all that well and there were tins of food everywhere that had been opened and left. My father was utterly distressed by the situation she'd found herself in. Then my brother arrived (the police inspector) and began to put some order into things. We found that she was quite well off – she'd left £15,000 in 1950, which would buy a three or four-bedroomed house in the suburbs of London! She'd risen in the Chilprufe Underwear Corporation, becoming a saleswoman then sales director. She'd gone to Spain in the 1930s (presumably to sell Chilprufe underwear), but she'd fallen in love with a Spanish officer, whose picture appeared in her diary, which was in her room. He was a very handsome man, and she said a lot about him. And then all of a sudden her remarks about him stopped. I turned the next page of the diary and across this two-page spread she'd written: 'The more I think of men, the more I love my dog.'

After that, she was with me and by my side. There was no way that I could not create a character based on her. In fact I based two characters on her: May in *Accrington Pals* and subsequently Mabel Cooper, a saleslady in *The Bright and Bold Design*.

The Bright and Bold Design comes near to home, to where I was born in Stoke-on-Trent, because it's about the pottery industry. And the police-inspector-of-facts' shadow fell across me and said, 'You should write a documentary play, about Clarice Cliff, the working-class painter who became a famous designer in the 1930s.' She used a very jazzy art-deco style, announcing the end of that gentler kind of Arts and Crafts movement of the Edwardian times. Crocus is the most famous one, on a yellow background, with the brush strokes making the design. It was very new at the time, and she became quite celebrated. Colly Shorter, who was the dashing director of the place (a man who rode to hounds and appeared at work in his hunting gear), took her up and sent her to art school in London, then to Paris to exhibitions.

And why was it that this was somehow too much for me? Why was it that I felt somehow I'd got too many facts? Why was it that I felt the story was too clean? I wanted desperately to interrupt it. I wanted to interrupt the story with something that cheated. So I thought, 'Why don't I take a woman like Clarice Cliff, but instead of wanting to rise and rise and become a star of commercial design, she has an ambition to paint landscapes, to paint trees, in the manner of Paul Nash.'

And so, having decided that, I needed a Svengali, I needed the director who she would come into conflict with. The answer was in my own family: again, somebody I'd never met – my wife's father. He was quite a considerable person in the Potteries. The reason I never met him was that he died in his forties of TB. He was a notable designer: his work is even now beginning to be discovered – Bristol Museum has an exhibition of it currently.

In the Potteries, he was also a notable socialist. He was chairman of the local party, and became the first president of the Society of Industrial Artists. Just after the war, he was about to move to London to become an adviser on industrial design to the Labour

Party – he knew some of the leading members of the party – but he died. He was a great arguer and public speaker, but he also loved fast cars: he had a Lancia in those days. He rented everything, believing you shouldn't own. He slept with a six-gun under his pillow, as he said, 'in case the revolution started in the middle of the night'. So, although he objected to being called a Red, he felt that if the revolution *was* going to start he might as well join in.

Also, very courageously, or foolishly, he gave a speech at lunchtime during the election of 1935, on how they should all vote Labour, which wasn't very clever because the Conservative candidate was a friend of the boss. So he got the sack and was blacked throughout the Potteries. He couldn't get work there any more and had to find work in Hereford and in Bristol (hence the exhibition of his work there).

Now, this man was almost too much for me. I thought, can I cope with this? But he was everything I required, the Svengali that my working-class heroine, Jessie Frost, has to oppose and tell, 'Look, no, I don't want to do cups and saucers with socialist designs of pylons and machinery and ocean liners and so forth on them. I want to paint landscapes.' Even though it's going to plunge her into poverty, she chooses to paint trees. So his character, as I received it, helped to write the play for me and I'm very grateful for that.

What I'm saying, I suppose, is that to me, embarking on a play is embarking on a mystery. I'll put it more strongly than that. I can only embark on a play if I'm absolutely convinced that I don't know what I'm doing. As the philosopher David Hume said, reason moves nothing. I can only go so far down the path of reason; something else has to take over. Therefore it seemed to me that in using members of my family I'd never met, a piece of the mystery remained. And I wasn't creating them alone. The people who knew them were helping to create them, which I also found an absolutely fascinating process. So, even though I freeze, I shall still prefer the string vest of partial knowledge to the warm shirt of total certainty.

To the writer who genuinely worries about using people in the family, I can offer no comfort whatsoever. You can't ask their permission: 'I've got this rather creepy character to put in my play – can I use you as a model?' I mean, you can't, can you? I can only say either don't do it, or only do it if you absolutely have to. But then, that's only what I'd say of writing itself – only do it if you have to.

Sebastian Barry

I made *The Steward of Christendom* with two things really: a pair of shirt studs from the 1930s that a friend found in an old house and that I put on my desk for a year to guide me, and an old childhood mental picture – childish vision, I would almost say – of a man riding on a high white horse against a mass of black-clothed strikers in Sackville Street: a man, it seemed, who was my own great-grandfather and who rose (as the singsong formulas of family histories go) as high as a Catholic could in the Dublin Metropolitan Police. Fellows like him don't figure in history books as names; they become part of the general story of the demonic nature of the times. In his case, the nameless demon who baton-charged Jim Larkin, arrested him and in the course of the catastrophic four minutes killed four good men and true on that day notorious in trades union history, notorious and emblematic, and in its own fashion true as daylight or not untrue.

The first time I heard about him, most likely from my mother, I saw him heroically, because I was a child and saw everything in heroic terms, on that white horse with a mane of sea foam, charging. More truly, he stood at the O'Connor monument in Sackville Street and ordered the baton charge as soon as Larkin appeared. The meeting was proscribed and illegal: it was his proper duty.

When I first considered this in the cold light of 1985, I was in fear of it being discovered that I had such a relative, hiding (you might say) in my very blood. I was eager to conceal him, indeed to keep him concealed, to seal him in, where he lay unnamed and unmentioned in official history. He was no cosy name around the fire of family, but a demon, a dark force, a figure to bring you literary ruin. What price my credentials as a real Irish writer?

A year or two later, struggling to be at home in my homeplace, I was embarked on a series of plays about forgotten, hidden people in my family, making them up more or less to create at least an imagined family for myself, and thereby an imagined self, an imagined country, taking the little shard of Fanny Hawke and making *Prayers of Sherkin* for her as an after-life, a heaven of sorts, taking the sharper fragment of Trooper O'Hara and giving him *White Woman Street* to ride about in. When I was embarked on this daft enterprise and four plays in, I felt in my bones, alas, that Chief Superintendent Dunne would have to have his goal, would have to be looked for, retrieved, the pattern of his broken plate restored as best I could. Because if it was joyful to try and rescue the benign figure of Fanny Hawke, didn't I have a responsibility to search out the demons too with the smoky, leaky, poor lamp of the imagination?

I did not even know his first name; I did not know really what had happened to him. There were no anecdotes to suggest him, no pictures or remnants of his life preserved. I think I was told that he said once, after independence in Ireland, 'My grandsons will be feral in this garden, mark my words.' It was the only line I had going into the play, and indeed, as the play stands, he no longer says it but reports another man saying it to him. 'My grandsons will be feral.' But I don't really know now if I made that up too.

Certainly the two most loved figures from my own childhood, Annie Dunne and Matthew Carling, or Barry as he was, who figure in the play, had been his daughter and his son-in-law. Certainly I knew well – as well as my own hat, if I had had a hat – the remote and tiny district of Kelsha and Kiltegan where the old policeman had been a child and where I had been a child a hundred or so years later. If nothing else, the play was an opportunity for me to see those beloved people once again as I imagined they might have been in their youth, but these few sticks are what I had to rub together to make the smoke of a first draft and hopefully at last the smoulder of a play.

And down into the moil of Thomas Dunne I went, lending him the first name of a close friend, lending him this and that, every damn thing I could lay my hands on to make him a world. My wife's great-aunt was just beginning the long adventure of Alzheimer's disease, and suddenly I remembered my old cousin Sarah Cullen, Annie Dunne's cousin too, who had looked after us heroically as children, and I remembered that Sarah had ended up in the county home in Baltinglass, homeless, blind and mad, where in the wild indifference of my twenties I had never dreamed of visiting her, much less rescuing her. And *mirabile dictu*, as soon as I put Thomas, my own imagined man, in that same institution – where indeed to my shame I had never been – the play began, actually began the way it begins now: 'Dada. Mama. Baba.' Not a blessed word could I get out of Thomas till he reached that terrible room, a site of attrition and forgiveness. Only there would he speak his life, open his trap, let me hear what he had to say for himself.

All the country stuff in the play was my own country stuff, you might say, from my childhood when I was four or so and staying with Annie and Sarah. I gave it to Thomas as the only gift I had for him. And after a bit I was inclined to give him gifts, as many as I had, because to my astonishment I slowly, slowly loved that diminished man. I was no longer looking for demons but trying to wrench a life from the dead grip of history and disgrace, to strike a bit of light into the forbidden room, to allow to a forgotten person not so much his history, which I did not know, but a story, all I had, made from the tangled string and bockety nails at my disposal. To every life an after-life, to every demon a fairy-tale. And if in the upshot I have made up my great-grandfather, by hook and by crook – well, I have made up myself too after a fashion. And there he abides in the play and I hardly know who he is, except he is familiar to me, he seems to be someone. And in the upshot, despite everything, because of everything, come hell or high water, I would stand at the gates of Saint Peter and claim my kinship clearly with that disgraceful, disgraceful man.

John Mortimer

I didn't have to take very great risks and live a dangerous and eventful life or fall out of trains, because the only risk I took was the considerable one of being born. And to be presented with my father, who was a person who had a most enormous influence on my life. He not only ejected me into life but he ejected me into drama. My father was a barrister, which is a sort of actor or dramatist, quite as free and easy with the truth as anybody else is. He also loved literature, knew all the Sherlock Holmes stories, and he knew all the plays of Shakespeare by heart, and he quoted them, as Rumpole quotes, at very inopportune moments. When I was four, every time my father (he could see then) caught sight of me, he used to say, 'Is execution done on Cawdor?' When you're four, that's a pretty tough question. And we used to go every year to see all the plays at what was then called, rather less pretentiously, the Shakespeare Memorial Theatre. We weren't the most popular members of the audience because my father liked a seven-course dinner, so we always arrived in the front row of the stalls about twenty minutes after the play had started. But once my father (who couldn't see by then) had had the set explained to him, he was of the most enormous assistance to the actors, because he could say all the lines at least five seconds before they could.

So there was I, the only child of this somewhat eccentric, blind father, who was very generous to me and gave me these wonderful lines. He did give me one of my best lines. He was doing these awful divorce cases in those days, when you had to prove adultery, cruelty and things like that. He used to come home to me in the nursery, sit on the end of my bed and tell me his triumphs in court. And he did actually say on one occasion, 'A terrific day in court today, John, managed to prove adultery by evidence of inclination and opportunity – and you know, really the only evidence we had was a pair of footprints upside down on the dashboard of an Austin 7 motor car outside Hampstead Garden Suburb.' Well, that was my father.

In time, because he was blind, my mother had to read all the awful evidence in all these divorce cases out loud. They used to travel up from Henley-on-Thames, where I now live, to Paddington and the divorce court, and there was my mother sitting in the first-class compartment of what was then called the Great Western Railway (and may still be called it again), and she had to read out these awful private detective reports about male and female clothing scattered around bedrooms in the Ritz hotel, stains on the bedsheets and so on. And by that time my father had grown deaf as well as blind: he'd say, 'Speak up, Cath!' She'd say '. . . stains on the bedsheet'. And the train would grind to a halt, and the entire first-class compartment would be absolutely silent, listening to the ever diminishing and ever more embarrassed tones of my mother in the faint hope of catching the name of some close friend.

So there was I, only child of a blind father who quoted Shakespeare at very inapposite moments and a mother who spent her time reading about stains on the bedsheets quietly to my father – so what could I do but tell lies to myself and perform plays? Because my father knew a lot of Shakespeare, I learnt it too. But I was an only child, so in *Hamlet* I had to duel with myself, make love to myself as my own mother, force myself to drink my own poisoned chalice, and the whole thing was quite a good training.

I decided to write a play about my father, to begin with because my father was the person who had most effect on my life, and also because I wanted to celebrate a sort of English middle-class professional generation which seems to have disappeared, when money was very unimportant – to talk about money was considered vulgar and obscene and stupid – and you actually did work and learn Shakespeare and enjoyed life. So I really wanted to celebrate that.

Is he a fictional figure or is he a factual figure? I think he was a fictional figure to himself to a great degree. Because he performed in court, pretended to be very angry when he wasn't angry at all, he pretended to be very shocked when he was quite unshockable, and when he was dying he got up and tried to have a bath and my mother tried to restrain him, thought he shouldn't get up, and my mother said to him, 'Don't be angry,' and he said, 'I'm always angry when I'm dying,' which is his last line in the play. Now, I bet anything you like that he'd thought that up for years and years. So what was he doing? Was he just dying, or was he acting at dying? I suppose to me the most frightening, alarming and vivid metaphor of a writer's life is that many years later, in that same bedroom where I'd sat watching my father die and hearing him say that, I sat with a film crew watching Laurence Olivier in my father's bed, with Alan Bates playing me, and me in the corner trying not to stand on the cable, and heard Laurence Olivier say in that bed and in that room, 'I'm always angry when I'm dying.' Now is that what we're all about? Do we go through the pain of life or the comedy of life in order to turn it back into fiction? Is it fact? I'm sure he said that, but there are many other lines in the play which I'm equally certain that he didn't say. Is that an obscene way of earning your living, or an awful way to live? My mother certainly thought it was: she would never see the play, because she thought it was almost as bad as talking about money or having a swimming pool, to write about your family and expose them to the public gaze, but I did it, have done it frequently. Is it art?

What effect does it have on us? Most people contain their own fathers, and people who haven't written such plays have still got their fathers inside them. My father has gone on, given out into the world to be almost a fictional character; he has been given away to the actors who've played him.

I can't imagine any writing which isn't really autobiographical. I remember that Ibsen said that Hedda Gabler was him, and if you think of this funny little man with wire glasses and a frock coat and an Order of the Norwegian first-class whatever with this beautiful woman who fired guns off and fell desperately in love ... that is what all fiction really is. You can't write emotions which you haven't experienced. I find it very difficult to write about places which I've never seen. So, autobiography, fiction, fact – it is all one strange amalgamation. We live, and we give it away again, and it goes out into the world. And what precise changes it's gone through I think are a matter of mystery.

Christopher Hampton's first success (*When did you last see my mother?*) was produced in the West End while he was still in his teens. His subsequent successes include *The Philanthropist*, *Savages* (both at the Royal Court), *Tales from Hollywood* (National Theatre) and an adaptation of *Les Liaisons Dangereuses* for the RSC which was subsequently filmed. A prolific and award-winning screenwriter and director, his autobiographical play *White Chameleon* was produced at the National Theatre in 1991.

Peter Whelan's plays *The Accrington Pals*, *Clay* and *The Bright and Bold Design* (all first produced by the RSC) draw on his extended family background in the Potteries. Further afield are the historical *Captain Swing*, *The School of Night* (about the death of Christopher Marlowe) and *The Herbal Bed* (about Shakespeare's daughter) for the RSC. His contemporary work includes the award-winning *Divine Right*, about the end of the monarchy (Birmingham Rep).

Sebastian Barry published seven books of prose and poetry before his play *Boss Grady's Boys* was performed on the Peacock Stage of the Abbey Theatre, Dublin, in 1988. Since then his plays include *Prayers of Sherkin*, *White Woman Street*, *The Only True History of Lizzie Finn*, the award-winning *The Steward of Christendom* and *Our Lady of Sligo*, many of which draw on his own family history.

John Mortimer's plays range from *The Dock Brief* to his RSC adaptation of *The Christmas Carol*; his television work includes the Rumpole series, many adaptations, and versions of his own novels *Paradise Postponed* and *Titmuss Regained*. His play about his blind barrister father (*A Voyage round My Father*) was originally written for radio, but subsequently produced on the stage and for television, starring Alec Guinness and Laurence Olivier respectively.

About That: Irish Plays

Bill Morrison, Anne Devlin, Conor McPherson

Bill Morrison

> History? I know about history. History always leaves out what
> people felt about it while it was happening. It always leaves out
> that most people didn't like it, didn't want it, protested about it,
> and were generally fucked up by it.
>
> Willy in *A Love Song for Ulster*

I'm in a very different situation from most playwrights in that if you
have a subject thrust upon you, then your work is defined by how you
react to that subject – how far you deal with it, how far you don't deal
with it. There are all kinds of legitimate ways for an Irish writer to
respond to Ireland, its history and its current situation. Oscar Wilde
had a most extreme response of one kind, which was to ignore the fact
that he was Irish at all. But I was twenty-nine in 1969, and so violence
became my subject whether I liked it or not. The choice was to
embrace the fact that this was happening, how you responded to it; it
had a great urgency about it to me. But it's how you respond to it that
then becomes the overriding question.

Now this is absurd, of course. Writers are far too peripheral. And
when events become so intense, so psychotic, it's very hard to know
where the writer stands in relation to this material, to this event, to the
thing that you know, that you see falling apart before you. I've
struggled a long time to define what the function of the writer is in
these circumstances, going back to the question of why is a writer
necessary to a society at all.

If you begin in the peasant economy and the village requires
everyone to have some kind of productive job which produces the
food that they need and the materials that they need to clothe
themselves and shelter themselves, then the writer is a luxury. But
when the village begins to have some kind of surplus, the first thing

that it does with the surplus is to hire a priest of some kind. Then of course it needs music: but that is supplied by the fact that all fiddlers are blind – that's how you can sustain your disabled within the Irish community. But the third element that occurs is what is called in Ireland the *seannachie*, the storyteller who moves from community to community carrying the tales and stories and the history. Of course the great danger of that is that the history becomes mythologized, and Ireland's stuffed with far too much of that.

But what is important, I think – going back to the quote from *Love Song for Ulster* – is the question of why, as soon as it has a little surplus, does society begin to have its storyteller? The reason is that it's only the writer who can tell you how people *felt* about it – that they didn't like it, didn't want it, protested about it and were generally fucked by it. It is only the writer who can ultimately carry forward a history of feeling. And that history of feeling becomes an essential counterbalance to the mythologizing, the propagandizing, which is the constant tendency of ruling structures.

And so I gradually found myself having to construct a form of history, and I feel that over a long period of time I have tried to document each stage of it, as it was experienced by people as opposed to how it has been told. And that seems to be a worthwhile function.

A couple of years ago I was invited to a writers' conference in Italy, broadly writers of the left, and it had writers from Israel, and Palestinians and Chileans, Paraguayans, Argentinians, Indians and so on. And I actually felt very embarrassed: I felt that I was there under false pretences, because nobody is going to put me in jail, nobody is going to remove my work from a bookshelf and burn it, nobody is going to torture me, nobody is going to oppress me, suppress me or any of those things.

But it did seem important to talk about why we all attempted to do theatre. I began in it as an actor, and the reason theatre became fascinating to me was that it was the only place I could find in the society I was growing up in that was ultimately a co-operative human activity, employing all the basic skills, the making of things, the weaving of things, the painting of things, the performing of things, the telling of stories, which ultimately work towards one co-operative end. And thus it doesn't matter what gender, gender preference, whatever, you are. It really does get down to that ultra-interdepend-ence, that when you are out on the stage with another performer, us and them and all the rest of it begins to disappear. And that seems to me the holy nature of theatre and its great importance, and I tried to express this to that conference.

But the other thing that seemed to me very important was expressed by the Israeli writer Joshua Sobol, who said about a play which had caused a great controversy (to his surprise): 'When I was writing it, I didn't know what I was doing.' And I said I thought that was extremely important, and it is true that none of us really, truly knows when we are writing what it is we are doing – it would be frightening if we did. But not knowing what you are doing is what makes us dangerous and what makes us important, because we are of necessity articulating things that have never been dreamt in quite that way before. That is why oppression, suppression of the writer and all the rest of it seem to me to occur. And it is that – the intellectual curiosity and the intellectual dreaming – which seems to me of great importance in trying to respond to the material. The other way in which you have to respond to the material is by being as rigorously honest as possible, and that goes along with the need to constantly re-examine history and the ways in which it is being retold.

My response was that if I wasn't willing to be active in this conflict – in other words, willing to take up a gun and use it – what weapon did I have? And it seemed to me that the only weapon I did have was jokes, that humour was of itself a most powerful and civilizing weapon; *The Times* did once say of me that I rolled in the jokes like hand grenades. And I thought, 'Yes, somebody knows what I'm trying to do.' I've always resisted the idea that Northern Ireland and the crisis of Northern Ireland is a tragedy. It isn't. It's tragic, but it is not a tragedy, because it is a chosen thing: people chose to pick up the gun, they chose to pull the trigger, they chose to do all these things. The responsibilities cannot be evaded. But it is tragic. And if it is tragic, then it is also comic, because the two are absolutely part of each other. And so the comic then becomes a defining form, and that has sustained me as a means of dealing with it all. I've not always done it that way – I have done more directly documentary things – but it has sustained me as a way of writing about it and of getting there.

Conor speaks of his memories of Bloody Sunday. He was eighteen months old and I was thirty-two. So Bloody Sunday for him is a distant history. While for me, the day after Bloody Sunday was the day which provoked many people in Northern Ireland – including most of the

Civil Service, an unheard-of thing – to walk out on strike for a day. And I was at that time resident writer in Stoke-on-Trent. And I sat all day all by myself in front of my typewriter refusing to type. Now there's the true position of the writer.

The following day I turned in my British passport, which I had simply because I was born a Protestant in Northern Ireland, and I became an Irish citizen, and therefore became a citizen of what was then one of the most socially repressive regimes in Europe.

It seemed an important thing to do, and it remains an important thing to do. At the same time, no play of mine has ever been performed in Ireland up until last year, in Belfast. Which is another element of being an Irish writer: while there is no longer censorship, there is a kind of indifference which occurs; you get marginalized in many ways. But I suppose the personal dilemma is always this: that I can look at a very considerable body of work and a career, and I have to say I wish I'd never written any of them, because I would rather the situation had never existed that made me write them in the first place.

Anne Devlin

I feel that I'm not at home in Ireland and I'm not at home in England, in the sense of where I should be and who I am writing for. I have this feeling that I go to places for a while and then I move on. At the same time I'm terrorized by what has been referred to as a collective history, a kind of collective experience of terror, of 'the terror', whatever that is.

In 1990, after I'd written the Birmingham Community Play *Heart-landers* with David Edgar and Stephen Bill, I'd been in England for fourteen years, and I took up a residency in Lund University in Sweden because I thought this would give me another perspective.

Before I went to Sweden I had a dream: this is very characteristic of the way I work when I'm trying to resolve something. I dreamt that I was climbing a hill above a village; the village was down at the coast. I looked back a couple of times at the village asleep in the early morning beside the bay. I was at the top, about to take my leave and disappear over the hill, when I finally looked back at the village and saw that the tall ships were in the bay, the long ships, the warships. And I had a choice before me: either to go on over the hill to safety and leave the village sleeping or to go down and wake then up and warn them that the Vikings had arrived. Of course I woke up at that point, before I resolved the dilemma.

And it felt very characteristic of my relationship with the country that I come from and with my history that I'd taken a particular choice, that having come to England I was making another departure. But until the point at which I was going to Scandinavia, it never occurred to me that I was collectively terrorized by the Vikings, that I was actually travelling towards the enemy, and I felt I had to explain this to the Swedes when I got there. And of course they immediately set about explaining to me that the Vikings were completely misunderstood, that they didn't have horned helmets (that was a misconception), that they were hungry sailors who didn't have the language and simply appeared on the coast looking for food. And people ran screaming at them, and set about them with weapons and so on. And so right away the whole thing shifted again for me.

And so in a way I think that's my dilemma as a writer. The reason why place is important is very simple; the reason why I started writing was to deal with events in my life in 1969, and that was lived, personal history. And when I first came to England I found myself completely removed from the sounds, from the voices that I had been used to hearing, the sounds of the community around me. And I never really felt I'd come from a community until I couldn't hear the sounds again. So every time we cast a play, when I hear those sounds, that seems to be a very important part of what I'm trying to reclaim. The play is an acoustic landscape.

And so the point about *Ourselves Alone* was that I was living in England, but I don't think I'd really left Ireland because in my head I was still there, and so I was creating those sounds that I needed to hear, and they were women's voices. So I decided to write a play about the women of Andersonstown, because we'd moved to Andersonstown out of the Falls Road, and indeed in 1969 the streets in which my father's family grew up were burnt to the ground. In the play I was looking very clearly at 'Am I a feminist? Am I republican?' – that choice between feminism and nationalism which haunts Irish history. And so there's that area, and there's also the whole business of how women live with war.

And then at the same time I really did make a departure: I did come to live in England very finally, because my son was born here. (I found

I was pregnant in the interval of *Ourselves Alone*.) And that changed my whole view of the work I was doing: I had a different relationship with the culture because my son, who is now twelve, was born here – a fact for which my mother (who doesn't claim to be a nationalist) has never really forgiven me. And so the plays are written to address my problem with the biography at a particular time. I fiercely say they're not biographical plays, because they are plays of experience, because they're in that gap between experience and biography. A biography is one life; experience is the knowledge of the stories of many who have touched your own. So they are also history plays and of course they are political plays too.

By the time I got to *After Easter*, which I wrote when I returned to England from Sweden, my whole constituency had changed because I'd really come to live here, because when you're educating children you live here, and also because I was absolutely convinced that I'd covered 1969 when I did *Naming the Names*. But it was a single woman without a family who'd written *Naming the Names*. What I feel about history's dynamic and continually changing relationship with me is that it continually surfaces. But it doesn't just surface for me; it surfaces for the next generation who've missed the context in which I had already dealt with it. So the point about writing *After Easter* was that I wanted to find a way in which I could explain my context to my son, the next generation ... and also to find a structure for myself through which I could say, yes I believe in that.

And it also has to do with the way the personality unravels without its boundaries, when the personality has a history that can continually trip it up: this is effectively what *After Easter* is about. That play was done in two countries – and I do see it like that – it was done here at the RSC and it was done in Belfast. Now the critics in Belfast didn't like it, but that didn't translate to the audiences: the theatre was packed. And it was controversial: there was a real sense that there were people who were going to talk to me about that play and there were people who weren't going to talk to me about that play. But as a dramatist I have to engage with that, I have to go home with the work and I have to be prepared not to be liked and I have to be prepared to be accused of betraying the tribe.

What I'm saying is that I have to keep moving – it's as if I can't put down roots, history won't let me. I do have a sense of a real absence of roots, but I think that's not just my experience. I think that every writer has had this experience with the communities that claim them. And I was very worried that, because of that absence of roots, I have come up with a proliferation of journeys, a proliferation of routes, which seems to me to be where I've got to now.

Conor McPherson

It is everywhere assumed that because I'm a playwright from Dublin in my twenties, I must be working in London. This assumption is correct. The main reason for this is that the population of Dublin is roughly a million, one-tenth of the size of greater London. Irish writers may moan about the lack of enthusiasm Dublin theatres show for their work – I've sat in pubs and shot my mouth off on this very issue. But the fact is that there simply isn't the market to sustain the steady stream of unknown playwrights.

Faced with the struggle to convince small audiences that a play is worth four times the price of a cinema ticket – and for a far riskier return – Dublin theatres react in one of two ways. The first is to rehash staple favourites over and again. One of Sean O'Casey's first three plays is a fairly safe bet; the audience know what they're getting. Throw in a few television actors and they'll come in their busloads.

The second is to adopt the moral high ground and identify the theatre audience as different from a mainstream cinema audience. Theatre becomes intellectual succour, something that is supposed to be good for you. But whatever chance an unknown playwright may have of scoring a popular hit in Dublin, the chance of scoring a popular, groundbreaking, intellectual *coup de théâtre* has got to be less. So unless you are secure in the knowledge that you can attract a large audience to see this unsolicited piece of work that's just landed on your desk at the Abbey or the Gate, you're disinclined to buy it.

The chances of attracting that audience are, of course, ten times greater in London. London has an audience for new writing. Newspapers and television programmes review new writing with enthusiasm. There are many awards for new writing. It has a profile and it sustains theatres.

For years I produced my own work in Dublin's smaller fringe venues. Then an agent from London saw one of my plays and took me on. Within about a month there was interest from the Royal Court and the Bush.

Overall, a new playwright in London is likely to earn around £4,000 for a play. Since this sum may have to last one or even two years, the writer will have to supplement the income. The new writing awards all have cash prizes. Or the agent may blag the writer a commission for a television or film screenplay.

But what you do get in London, and promptly, is the attention of the press. Your play comes under rigorous scrutiny in a score of publications. And whatever your opinion of theatre criticism and theatre critics, if you don't get good reviews, people don't come.

In London I found that I was identified as belonging to two completely different schools. The first was the twentysomething playwrights who have recently had such media attention. But I was also slotted into the so-called school of Irish writing which seemed to be 'flooding' London theatres.

Although I had never set out to write consciously about my country, my work seemed to suggest Irish issues to certain critics. One reviewer saw *This Lime Tree Bower* – a series of monologues featuring a disenchanted philosophy professor and two Dublin brothers – as inescapably set against a backdrop of the conflict in the North. Another went so far as to describe *The Weir* – four Irishmen telling ghost stories in a country pub – as 'a requiem for Ireland'.

This may be true for some people, but all I was trying to do was to write plays that hold your attention, make you laugh and hopefully engender a sense of community between the work and the audience. I wasn't concerned with geography or politics. I am from the Republic of Ireland and that's where my plays have their genesis, but not from any need to address anything about my country. My nationality, however, forms the context in which I'm reviewed. And in London, being Irish has a resonance that being, say, Danish doesn't.

People of my age grew up with a confused detachment from the violence in Ireland. My first memory of the conflict was my mother explaining an item on the news where people had been murdered in a bomb attack. She said something about an army, the Irish Republican Army. She said her father had fought in the army when it was a real army. But now it wasn't a real army any more.

When I was a young boy, the H-Block hunger strikes took place. For weeks, possibly months, my dad promised my older sister and I that he would take us to the zoo next Saturday if the weather was fine, or to the pictures if it was raining, and when it came around and we asked him, he always said, 'I said next Saturday.' But eventually it was this Saturday, and we all set out for that kind of day of intense enjoyment that only children expect. And as we set out the weather was good, so we were going to the zoo, but it must have turned bad because we went to the pictures, and we went to the Plaza in Parnell Square, and when we emerged it was into the preparations for a Republican march. Our car was blocked by one of the coaches that had transported people down from the North for the day. My father was annoyed. He lifted me and my sister on to a wall, clinging to the railings, while he went to find the driver.

I'll never forget the scene around me. The first thing that struck us, besides the huge amount of people, was the din. Marching bands pounded lambeg drums and snare drums, a sound which you have to hear live to appreciate its terrifying, macabre attraction. Pictures of the hunger strikers were on banners all around us. The faces were blurred, blown up from group photos. They were smiling. Out for the night. Years ago. Nearly all had beards and long hair. People my age still equate those images with the pictures of Jesus in our school books.

On other banners was what I can only describe as an artist's impression of a prisoner, the generic hunger striker. It was done in simple black lines, an almost skeletal figure reclining on his back, long hair, beard and blanket to reflect the dirty protest and refusal to wear prison uniforms, which was what they died for. There were large depictions of barbed wire with blood dripping off it and hundreds of black flags.

To a child, this all seemed nightmarish. I was scared. But my father's dismissal of the whole spectacle in his bid to find the coach driver also shaped the way that I felt. His attitude was that it was nothing to do with us. All the more reason to be annoyed that we were hemmed in and couldn't drive away. This was not anti-Republican. It was anti-The Whole State of Affairs, British and Irish.

This attitude in the Republic is allied to a feeling of helplessness or impotence in the face of so much bitterness. We know the facts and the grievances on both sides. But we don't understand how that feels. We owe our independence to the men and women who gave their lives and to their families who lost them, but we're often not sure how to think about them. Do we dwell on the great injustices they suffered and become increasingly upset about something we can never really make right? Or do we simply embrace the future they've secured for us? Which is the best way to honour them?

This incomprehension of political violence is reflected in the attitudes of characters in the plays of my Dublin contemporaries. In Declan Hughes's *Halloween Night*, nationalists on the television news are referred to as the 'bearded weirdos in the woolly jumpers'. In *Digging for Fire* someone jadedly implores, 'Oh, spare me *the North.*' A character from Enda Walsh's *Disco Pigs* reflects the sort of taxi-driver philosophy so prevalent in the Republic: 'No one gis a fuck aboud dem nordy bas-turds. Way bodder? News a da wek is let dem do each odder in!'

But equally there are dramatists who tackle the conflict head on. The Peacock in Dublin recently staged Gary Mitchell's play about loyalist paramilitaries, *In a Little World of Our Own*. But Gary is from Belfast and the situation is obviously much more present for him.

The world is, of course, aware of the work Jim Sheridan and Neil Jordan have done in films such as *In the Name of the Father*, *Some Mother's Son* and *Michael Collins*. But to form your political convictions from works which have necessarily been fictionalized for the purposes of entertainment is as misguided as basing your opinion on the banners and flags I saw that day in Parnell Square.

Like my dad, I just want to get the car out. I will never address that conflict in my work. My father remembers where he was on Bloody Sunday because I had whooping cough and he sat up with me all night. I was a baby and this was the beginning of an unfortunate calendar we've come to mark our terrible days upon. But I was only a boy, and all I know is that years later I went to London with my plays when I wasn't having a lot of luck in Dublin. And I was made welcome. And I'm grateful for it.

Bill Morrison was born in County Antrim into a Presbyterian family. He was associate and then artistic director of the Liverpool Playhouse from 1981–5, with Chris Bond, Willy Russell and Alan Bleasdale. His stage plays include an adaptation of *Tess of the d'Urbervilles* (Stoke), *Patrick's Day* (Long Wharf, New Haven), *Flying Blind* (Everyman, Liverpool, then the Royal Court, London, and New York), *Scrap* (Liverpool Playhouse, then Half Moon Theatre, London), and the trilogy *A Love Song for Ulster* for the Tricycle Theatre, London.

Anne Devlin comes from West Belfast, and has dealt with the conflict in Ireland in her stage plays *Ourselves Alone* (Liverpool Playhouse and Royal Court) and *After Easter* (RSC) and her television plays *The Long March* (BBC1) and *Naming the Names* (BBC2).

Conor McPherson was born in Dublin; his plays include *Rum & Vodka, The Good Thief, This Lime Tree Bower, St Nicholas* (performed by Brian Cox at the Bush Theatre, London, in 1997) and the award-winning *The Weir*, which opened at the Royal Court in 1997 and has been revived twice at the same theatre.

Warning Shots
Nicholas Wright, Mike Bradwell

Nicholas Wright

> What I do, I get out of the air. Even if it's not so hot always, I put
> my little hand out there in that void, there, empty air. Look at it.
> It's like being a bleeding conjuror with no white tie and tails.
> Air ... It never pays what it costs.
> John Osborne, *The Hotel in Amsterdam*

For a playwright to talk with any clarity about writing requires an act
of wrenching, of splitting yourself in two, of standing apart from
what's probably most important about yourself. It can be done – it isn't
even very difficult – but I think it's valuable to recognize, when you
perform it, that the divide is there: that the politician in you is observing
and perhaps at the same moment robbing energy from the poet in you.
That the yogi has, however briefly, been displaced by the commissar.

I'm very used to this process, having spent so much of my life not
writing plays but advising people about them, directing them and
writing about plays of the present or past. It still says 'playwright' on
my passport, but if anybody was to suggest that 'stalled' or even
'ex-'playwright was more accurate I wouldn't say they were being
unkind (though of course they'd be being very unkind indeed): I'd see
some merit in it.

I do the work I do because I enjoy it. But you can take it from me
that it isn't helpful to the more private process known as writing. And
writing is what I want to talk about for the next few minutes. I don't
mean genre writing, or adapting or writing in any way to order. I mean
going a little bit mad within yourself, while perhaps remaining sane on
the outside. Mad in the sense that you're following an obsession, one
you have fallen victim to for reasons you probably can't explain, one
which will never be of any real interest to anyone else at all unless they
are persuaded by you of its power and individuality.

To make it a little bit more specific, I'm going to talk about some of the enemies of writing.

The first is success, both one's own success and the success of others. People keep contrasting the blown-up successes of today and the supposedly more authentic ones of the early Royal Court days, and I can perhaps add something to this. It's hard to realize, if you weren't there, how very parochial the London of the 1950s and 1960s was. There were, if I remember, only six decent bookshops, and I'm including Foyles. When I first came to London the only way of meeting the kind of people you wanted to know was spending three days walking from Aldermaston to London. And there was – this is important – very, very little arts coverage. Even in the 1960s and early 1970s, when I started putting on plays in the Theatre Upstairs, you got the reviews the next day and then you got another three on Sunday, then the next week you got *Time Out* and that was more or less it, until a month later *Plays and Players* delivered what in those days was considered a magisterial clincher.

But there were no profiles, no listings apart from *Time Out*, no appearances on TV, no round-ups of the week, no briefings, no Pass Notes. So, though there were indeed theatrical celebrities, there were fewer of them and the quality of their fame was different.

What happened to change all this was a realization in which, for better or worse, I played some part. Which was that, even if a play went on to only sixty people – this being a full house in the Theatre Upstairs, compared to four hundred in the Theatre Downstairs or eight hundred or more in a West End theatre – it got the same amount of media coverage, the same quantity and size of reviews and the identical public impact as if the play had been produced in a full-scale theatre. And very strangely, the number of people who *thought* they'd seen the play, or who at the very least thought of themselves as participants in its success, was also the same.

This was a major cause of the immense proliferation of coverage, disposable coverage, which has now proved such a burden for successful young writers.

It's a burden because if you are being rewarded for a success which you achieved partly or largely by accident, you know all too well that there's no guarantee that you'll ever be able to do it again. This feeds a neurotic fear of failure, which is in itself a great enemy of writing. Besides, when the temperature is hotter, the produce tends to go off faster, so that six months later you risk the humiliation of being out of a fashion which you can't even pretend to despise since you so clearly enjoyed it while it was smiling on you.

All this combines to breed envy of other writers, which is the second enemy of writing and on which there is no need to enlarge.

The third enemy is help. The race is on to discover new writers, and any theatrical institution which neglects to do so or scores too many conspicuous misses will soon find itself roundly attacked, with all the consequent damage to its ego and its funding. One result of this is that too many playwrights are given too public a platform too soon. This is helpful for gifted talent spotters because talent, in my view, nearly always makes itself apparent in a writer's earliest work. But skill and craft don't. I often remember that Caryl Churchill, for example, wrote about ten plays for the theatre before her first was ever produced: she sustained her self-identity meanwhile by writing short radio plays (BBC Radio Drama was in those days an enlightened patron). Edward Bond wrote something like twelve stage plays before *The Pope's Wedding*. Martin McDonagh, who has so surprised everyone with his mature technique, wrote over twenty radio plays, all rejected, before any of his plays for the theatre hit the stage. Of course, to write a play and have it rejected, and to put it in a drawer before starting the next one, isn't a pleasant experience. But if you know how to use it, it's an educative one, on which too many writers are missing out. Far too many writers are being persuaded or coerced into rewriting plays which should in fact be put down to experience, purely because a theatre which should have rejected a play – and plainly doesn't have very much confidence in it – has kept the writer dangling with suggestions of a rehearsed reading or a production if the next-but-one rewrite comes up trumps.

I use the word 'help' in a playful sense because few things can be more genuinely helpful than the attention of a skilled and sympathetic literary manager. But this is rare. Lovers and loyal friends make a good substitute. Bad help is a calamitous enemy and I expect it to be more common in the future. As management culture seeps into every level of our lives, so will dramaturgical help become more managed and more intrusive. Writers will be asked for more and more detailed treatments, then those treatments themselves will become subject to rewrites, and so on. The only advice I can give to any victim of this kind of attention is to take the money and lie your socks off. Because this situation is irrevocable.

Old age is an enemy, or has for a long time been considered so, and so it's very cheering to note that this is clearly changing, along with so many other things about old age. Peter Whelan is writing more fruitfully than he has ever done before, I think, at the age of sixty-five. Sophocles did the same at *eighty*-five. This is worth remembering, though I'm sure most of you think it will never happen.

A great enemy of – or problem with – writing can be Englishness. By this I don't – and I seriously don't – mean to suggest there is anything etiolated or inartistic in the English temperament. I mean that the notion of Englishness and the symbols or icons of Englishness which define it have for a variety of historical reasons been degraded, so that the English artist does not have recourse to them in the way that people from many cultures do.

I'd never thought of this until the recent political changes in my home country, South Africa. I now have an experience which I would never have dreamt possible: that of being very emotional at the sound of the national anthem, deeply proud of the head of state and very attached to the flag, a miniature example of which I wear on my key ring. That's inconceivable with the Union Jack. This experience has encouraged me to think about how, as an artist, it's necessary to be in touch with your own culture, and if that culture is English culture I think that is quite a difficult thing to do.

There's been much talk of the way in which Irish playwrights have sustained the English theatre, and the only thing I would argue with here is that the word 'always' has a tendency to creep in, quite inaccurately. There were no Irish playwrights writing in England in the Jacobean or the Elizabethan eras. Their contribution dates from the Restoration: that calamity which effectively disowned the visionary puritanism of Shakespeare, Webster and Middleton and silenced almost every English playwright of the first rank until the advent of Granville-Baker over two hundred years later.

The Irish filled the vacuum uninhibitedly: without them, English theatre would have died. In the present century, the baton was seized by gay male playwrights whose talent was for the coded and the oblique, or Northerners who saw it through a class perspective: Lawrence, the Manchester writers and, later, David Storey. Osborne struck Englishness in C major: not to my ear an attractive key. The right one remains elusive.

Number six: a serious enemy of new writing is the myth that people won't come and see it. In 1601, when the Earl of Essex planned a revolt against Elizabeth I, his allies asked the Lord Chamberlain's Men – Shakespeare's company – to stage a revival of *Richard II*, because they hoped the deposition scene might incite the citizens of London to rise up in Essex's support. The company refused. They said it was a mouldy play, many years old, and that 'if we perform it we will have little or no company'. They absolutely assumed that if you did an old play people wouldn't come to see it, exactly as a cinema owner today would rather show a new Harrison Ford movie than a ten-year-old one. The Lord Chamberlain's men were in fact persuaded to do the mouldy play by a payment of forty shillings, which made up for the box office deficit. It's obviously the case that too many theatres now are being given the metaphorical forty shillings for putting on old plays. That's a campaigning point worth mentioning.

The seventh enemy of writing is the one I feel strongest about. The collapse of small theatres, not just in London but regionally, has been a catastrophe. Almost all first plays will be done in a studio theatre, for the simple reason that, although the productions are bound to lose money, that amount is finite and can be budgeted for in advance. The often-debated question of how a writer escapes from the studio theatre into a big one seems to me to be a secondary question, one which will finally best be solved by writers themselves in the light of what they see when their plays are produced – on however small a scale – in what used to be called 'a first-class manner': well cast, well publicized, well directed.

What counts is the first production. For decades I've insisted that a good play by a new writer will almost certainly be produced because somewhere or other there is a theatre which needs it. This is now a lie. The theatres no longer exist. Good plays are being lost: they might as well be left out on the pavement in bin-bags. This is my final campaigning point.

Mike Bradwell

This is going to be metrocentric but I run the Bush Theatre, which is in London, and I have the best job in the world. I can put on what plays I want, when I want, with who I want in them, and I do plays that are good: that's the only criteria I've got – there's no other agenda. I believe in the Bill Shankly principle of theatre, which is that it's not a matter of life and death, it's much more important than that. And I think new writing is what it's all about.

I'm not convinced there is any new writing renaissance at the moment; I think there's a renaissance in talking about new writing, but that's not the same thing. I'm worried about the fashionable nature of it: not because it's not great that new writing's being celebrated in the way that it is, but because if we think theatre writing's the new rock 'n' roll, it could go the way of Haircut 100 and the hula hoop. It might be last year's model, and I don't want that. And I also think we can be seduced into thinking we're safe, that there's an awful lot of people interested in what we do and we are the DNA of the nation. In fact, the size of our congregation is pretty small. I still have a theatre that seats a hundred people, it's not always full and there are ten million people in London.

We do get a tremendous amount of coverage in the newspapers for what we do and I'm very pleased about it; though if people realized there's only a hundred people going nightly into the Bush, they might stop giving us that coverage. And I think that's very possible, the way things are going.

I always used to say, and I still say it – I don't know why, because it's sentimental bollocks – that the great thing about the Bush Theatre was that it was in a pub, and you go down those twenty steps and there are a whole bunch of people who don't give a shit about what you do upstairs. And what it does for me is to give me some kind of sense of perspective; and if you work in the theatre, where all you do is theatre all the time, you don't have any sense of what the man in the street is thinking or doing.

Well, let me tell you it's not that great. We've just been refurbished at the Bush and it's interesting what's happened in terms of what people really think about theatre and of how theatre and what we do is perceived. Because the Bush has now become the Fringe and Firkin, and the Fringe part is supposed to be because it's a fringe theatre (it's not a homage to pelmets). And so somebody came up from Firkin headquarters, the people who did branding, and they worked out what you had to have in a Firkin pub. All Firkin pubs are alliterative, so if you have a Photographer and Firkin, you get a load of old cameras. The Fringe and Firkin really stumped them. But they thought, 'Oh, theatre', so what they came up with is a pantomime cow, a set of bongo drums and a cartoon of Hamlet drinking draught bitter. That is what people think fringe theatre is all about. Most people who don't have an opinion about what we do think basically that's what it's all at. There's also an awful lot of slogans: 'Shakespeare married an Avon Lady', 'Shakespeare got the idea of Hamlet from Bacon'; there's another one that says, 'Before you gag, buy the Firkin bag,' and it's got a cartoon of Hamlet being sick in it. Right? So this gives you some idea.

Also, what they did was introduce this range of beers. Shakesbeer was one of them; Thespian's Revenge was another one; and the best of all was Luvvy Ale. Luvvy Ale. So we thought, 'Oh, fuck this,' and we got on to Firkin headquarters and we got Mr Firkin. We said, 'Look, do you realize that "luvvy" is a term of abuse?' And he said, 'Well, you're a bunch of humourless tossers. It's just an example of our quirky sense of humour.' And maybe, yes, we do sometimes get an over-inflated idea of the importance of what we do.

Now, the Fringe and Firkin is quite close to the BBC, and the other night I was having a drink there and probably talking about this. There were two script editors from the BBC series and serials; they were in their late twenties and they were with somebody I knew who used to work at the Bush. And these script editors said that they never went to the theatre in their lives because they hated it and they thought it was rubbish, because you couldn't talk through it and it was too much like hard work. One of them said they didn't like theatre because what TV does is find out what people want and give it to them, and what we do is preach to people and that makes theatre undemocratic. That was two people from the BBC.

This connects with the *Late Show* people, Tony Parsons, cultural studies, the post-modernists, all writing articles about how basically they'd rather get a video. And underneath it is to do with (a) fashion and (b) the lack of any moral rigour about what they think and what they believe. While in theatre, you have to examine who you are and why you do things to people and why we talk to each other like we do and why we behave in the ways that we do, and that's what it's about. But if you think you're the most fashionable person in the world, you don't care about any of that stuff.

I think we're really in danger now – and I don't think the Labour government is going to help. A deputation of directors went to see Mark Fisher to talk about the Labour Party arts policy document, which when we got there hadn't come out, because first Gordon Brown had taken it back to make sure it didn't promise anything, and then Tony Blair had taken it back to make sure it didn't say anything.

To nick a term from the Firkin headquarters, what we've got to do in theatre – I'm serious about this – is to reposition the brand. We've got to stop going, 'Ooh, it's a big risk to put on new plays.' We've actually got to be very, very clear about what it is that we do and why we want to do it. Maybe we can get Lottery money so that new writing is not going to be more expensive than old writing. And I want to see new work being at least fifty per cent of the work in all theatres' main houses from now on. I'd like to have a one-year embargo on Shakespeare. And I'd like to get back to London so I can get on with it.

Nicholas Wright was the first director of the Royal Court Theatre Upstairs, joint artistic director of the Court 1975–7, then literary manager of the National Theatre, and subsequently associate director. His plays include *Treetops* and *One Fine Day* (Riverside Studios), *The Gorky Brigade* (Royal Court), *The Crimes of Vautrin* (Joint Stock), *The Custom of the Country* and *Desert Air* (RSC), a version of Pirandello's *Six Characters in Search of an Author* and the play *Mrs Klein* (both at the National) and a version of Pirandello's *Naked* (Almeida). His writing on theatre includes *99 Plays*.

Mike Bradwell founded Hull Truck Theatre Company in 1971, devising and directing work by the company and also Doug Lucie, Alan Williams and Peter Tinniswood. He has directed twenty-five shows at the Bush Theatre, including plays by Terry Johnson, Catherine Johnson and Bill Tidy and Alan Plater. In 1996 he became artistic director of the Bush; his own productions include Joe Penhall's *Love and Understanding*, Doug Lucie's *Love you, too* and Catherine Johnson's *Shang-a-Lang*.

Back to the Future

David Eldridge, Dusty Hughes

David Eldridge

> Starting in 1994, continuing through 1995 and 1996, a remarkable
> number of striking young playwrights emerged in England ...
> Their ages ranged from twenty-four to thirty-four, and they had
> much in common. Their characters drifted around weird
> cityscapes, where violence was a frequent threat and escape from
> feelings of entrapment mostly an illusion. But unlike their
> predecessors, these dramatists had no obvious ideology, no
> political credo, no social agenda. If their characters launched into
> generalization, it was more likely to be about drinks and drugs
> than the sins of the Establishment. They observed the urban
> British quizzically, reported the contradictions they saw, and left
> the audience to reach its own conclusions.
> Benedict Nightingale, *The Future of Theatre* (Phoenix, 1998)

There is a perception of theatre and new writing at the moment, I
think, which is jointly manufactured by some of us in the London new
writing scene and by others in the press and media, that it's trendy to
go and see new plays again. So-called *Trainspotting*-generation
writers like myself, Mark Ravenhill and Jez Butterworth, amongst
many others, have apparently attracted a new audience of fucked-off,
E-taking twentysomethings.

But I have to say, this isn't a perception I share of my own writing
and its impact. It isn't a perception which I think is wholly represen-
tative of the rich vein of new drama which has been written and
produced over the last two or three years, and when I hear phrases like
'the drama of disenchantment' uttered gravely by critics and commentators I feel like keeling over.

Of course, it is clear that there have been a raft of plays: a lot of
them by younger men, with not always enough parts for women, some

of which are angry, some of which depict disturbing sexual and violent imagery and incidents, and some of which are About Now.

In the nineteen months since I first put my occupation down as playwright, I've known nothing other than the current healthy state of new writing in London. But others tell me this wasn't always the case, so it's easy to understand why this new-found trendiness is being trumpeted to the rafters. And it is brilliant and exciting to see theatres with younger, less traditional theatre audiences, but I just think we're kidding ourselves a bit about what's really going on. As far as I can see, our new audience is a largely upwardly mobile twentysomething group which might drop *Generation X* into the conversation over a bottle of Beck's in the bar before the show, but they're far more likely to have a copy of the *Evening Standard* to hand than Douglas Coupland's slacker bible. This younger audience, many my age, might well be taking any number of recreational drugs on the weekend, but they couldn't possibly consume the boxloads of E, speed and smack that the characters on stage do, as they've all got jobs to keep down. I'm certainly not taking as many drugs as some of the characters I've written do. In fact, I'm not taking any drugs at all.

And if you look closer at the work of the so-called *Trainspotting*-Tarantino influenced generation of writers that I'm bunched in with, I think it's much richer than we're given credit for. I can't imagine a much fiercer attack on consumerism and late capitalism than Mark Ravenhill's *Shopping and Fucking*. And forget the controversy, what about Sarah Kane's classical poetic vision? Much was made of Jez Butterworth's Tarantino-like dialogue, but my parents testify to the accuracy of the glitter-and-grime escapism of 1950s rocking-and-rolling. For myself, I always saw my play *Serving it Up* as a play as much about disaffected middle age as youth. My more recent plays have been about north London Tories and Thatcher's children in the suburbs. This may sound boring but I prefer Robert Holman to Quentin Tarantino, I thumb *Middlemarch* more regularly than I do *Trainspotting*, and I'm much more likely to take a copy of *The Whitsun Weddings* than *Loaded* magazine into the loo for a read.

I don't programme plays. I write them. But I'm anxious that we should all be wary about the growing sense of fashion consciousness I detect. I'm not saying that the theatre is in thrall to fashion now, but I think we're at a crossroads. With many of the older generation of theatre critics and commentators' feet firmly pointed backwards, there seems to be a mission either to recreate the spirit of 1956, or 1968, or to defend to the death that creaking old dinosaur, the tub-thumping plot. Some of the younger critics' priorities seem to lie in cutting their journalistic teeth by blooding newer dramatists rather than reviewing plays properly. Throw in this growing sense of riding an exceptionally cool wave, and we're at an odd situation where sexy first plays are praised beyond belief, second and third plays by new writers get surface treatment, and most bizarrely of all, anything written by anyone who has a reputation already, or is doing anything perceived as remotely different, is written out of the excitement.

This probably sounds more like I'm shitting on my own doorstep than Trumpeting the Zeitgeist, but the theatre that I want to be part of should, I think, be as broadly diverse as it is rich in depth, as much about diversity of form as it is about content; plays fired by ideas sitting alongside those with no inclination other than to tell us a good story. Where social realism jostles for a slot with exciting new work from abroad. A season of new works which might include myself and any of my fellow panellists. This is the theatre I want to be part of. Rich new writing that is genuinely popular but avoids a style-conscious populism, taking risks but remaining unpretentious, a theatre where new voices are embraced and nurtured, rather than exalted and then rejected. This is the theatre that I want to be part of for life. I don't want to be part of something that's out of fashion in twelve months' time.

The most significant development of the last three years or so is, I think, the large-scale rejection of the clonky old form of what's-round-the-corner plotting. Of course, some commentators interpret this as a neutered or incomplete form of drama, but really it's just a different sort of writing – a different form of drama. They think we find plot hard. I don't mean to sound flippant, but I think it's the reverse. Plots are relatively easy. You work out the end of the play and work backwards. Carefully shading a character, writing rich dialogue, developing a character's story line by line, on the line, and trusting the imaginative impulse – all of these things are much harder than Meccano-building a plot. Our audiences are engaging with these newer approaches, but of course this is far less sexy copy than trumpeting or denouncing the new generation of Angry Young Men and Women. Similarly, we had a frank exchange of views from

Michael Billington and Stephen Daldry about whether the big state-of-the-nation play is a vital point at which new writers earn their spurs. Fine. They're entitled to their opinions, but I think they both miss the real issue at stake. If we want to write plays with bigger casts or for bigger stages, there aren't always the opportunities to do so any more. Surely this is much more important than a narrow debate about the content?

If I want to write a play for a bigger stage or for more characters than seven or eight, where do I take it apart from the National or the RSC? I feel that all around us there are voices, opinion formers and artists with axes to grind who are talking about the plays that are being written but sound dangerously like they're telling us what plays we should write. I think they should be a little less vocal and let the playwrights get on with their job. Our plays simply speak for themselves.

Dusty Hughes

The thesis put forward for discussion by this conference is that there has been a swapping of identities between television drama and the theatre. In this ideal world, always on the point of transforming itself into a golden age, we have a vibrant popular television that airs social issues and taboos in even its least ambitious soaps, reaching and transforming the viewpoint of its audience. And we have a theatre with its finger on the zeitgeist, or perhaps even up it, which combines gritty social realism with resonant characterization. But is that really the case? Leaving aside the creepy *doppelgänger* aspect of this identity swap, is it not true to say that, like everything else, both have felt the cool breeze of market forces in the air?

At the moment both television and stage share an obsession with violence and death. I believe this reflects something of society's insecurity at the end of the millennium. Detective series and hospital dramas and the pathological dramas that are a bit of both now dominate television drama to an almost ludicrous degree. Television reflects a society that is obsessed with violent death and disease. Few people can now ignore the possibility of a sudden end to happiness: a redundancy, a termination of contract, a leaving of home. This lurking doom is the murder that happens pre-titles or the body under the patio on a Liverpool estate.

Television has become Jacobean, and stage drama is well on the way back there. Unless, as the director of the Royal Court has recently said, it is just one more fashion.

Nevertheless, I am convinced that theatre and television are becoming more and more alike in their preoccupations. You might say the tail was wagging the dog, except that the theatre threatens to become the tail and television the hound. And all this is the result of a medley of influences in the last fifteen years, not just the way we live now, but a turning away perhaps from the smugness of political drama, a distinctly anti-intellectual atmosphere, a recognition by writers of the economic realities, and a slightly decadent interest in the gothic.

Violent death is very comforting in the form which is allowed on television (and which it does so well). Death is cool and matter of fact. It happened before we came on the scene to someone else, somewhere else. Apart from the odd prison throat-slitting, the essence of death on television is often now revealed in the lingering shots of body parts, on the mortuary slab and in the cooler in *McCallum* and *Silent Witness* and *The Ice House*, accepted these days without comment or much fuss. But unlike the Jacobean theatre, television has taken the horror out of horror. It is never pretentious. The television controllers who encourage the meat market know they are not flirting with social disgrace.

It would be interesting to compare television's mortuary slab with the fate of Anthony Noel Kelly, recently tried, convicted and imprisoned in connection with the disappearance of body parts from the dissecting room of a teaching hospital. Noel Kelly is a sculptor and, like Leonardo, has to acquire his raw material in an underhand way. He is an artist and a freak, and fair game to be called a pervert by the newspapers. He has already been jailed, but an even worse fate might await him: he might become the subject of a three-part fact-based drama serial. For his is not a publicly sanctioned story.

If Anthony Noel Kelly was in a procedural thriller, he would not be the misunderstood victim of a witch hunt, but the hunted and loathsome outcast: the Prime Suspect.

We are living in an era when cultural boundaries are being broken down, particularly between posh art and popular culture. This is not something that everybody finds comfortable. The very fact that you can now watch art movies at home on your video robs them of some of the mystique that memory once gave them. They are never quite as good as you thought.

But *EastEnders* is culture, there's little doubt of that, and it is both hugely enjoyable and true to life. In one sense it is essential, but in another sense it isn't drama at all, because since it never ends it never ultimately delivers any meaning. It is very dramatic, but when you think about it (which to be honest it doesn't really invite), it is always unsatisfying. When a character comes to the end of her personal journey in a soap, it never quite feels like the end of a proper story. It is only a strand in a format which is already stripped and stranded by the script editors.

What we have here is at the heart of drama on television. Enormously vital and consumptive of talent, but largely hidebound. The great trap of television is that drama isn't really in the hands of writers at all. It is in the hands of controllers and development executives and script editors. What begins as intelligent structure ends as leaden formula.

In the last two years I confess to having been responsible for three-and-a-half hours of fairly mediocre television drama and two hours that I could justifiably feel proud of. Although I know it seems like a cowardly defence, I would say that I was only as good as I was allowed to be.

In one case – a new medical series – a small team of personable writers was assembled to try and achieve a kind of British *ER*: fast moving, interestingly shot, at the sharp end of medicine, confrontational, crazy, ethical and moral. After a couple of meetings the writers disappeared to various corners of England (that was the first mistake) and set to work.

The script editor and producer now started to feel they were losing control, and simultaneously the Network Broadcaster started to lean on the Independent Producer to make the series more like a cross between *London's Burning* and *Casualty*, thus apparently assuring a gigantic audience. Gradually the demand for compromises started to filter through. The writers had been engaged on false pretences, and gradually the characters were asked to become duller, the events to be more predictable and the medical jargon more indecipherable. Your correspondent hung on, thinking of his wardrobe, his dinners in Granita and his *lebensraum*. As the characters got duller, the casting got prettier. The whole series did far better than it deserved to, pulling in at least nine million viewers. But coming in below the network centre's magic ten million, it was mercifully put to sleep after one series.

On the credit side, I was engaged to write the final ever episodes of a first-rate BBC series (*Between the Lines*) which was coming to the end of its natural life. The Independent Producer gave me *carte blanche* to write a two-hour drama that both resolved the characters we had all grown to know and combine it with a big political theme of contemporary relevance. I was able to write about the paranoia of our security services in the post-Cold-War era and their tendency to dangerous and incompetent political interference. More importantly, I was able to write about the rise of fascism in Europe and invade a real neo-Nazi rally in Belgium.

I was able to resolve the fate of one well-known chain-smoking character, who found his nemesis with a final cigarette butt. There was enthusiasm, constructive criticism and the text was treated with respect. It was superbly directed by Roy Battersby and it is something I am proud of.

But then, being as it were the death of the series, there was nothing at stake except satisfying story telling and artistic integrity. The viewing figures held up nicely.

Television now describes our values for us. It sees how far it can go, pushing gently, pulling back if confronted, but always looking to make a splash. What the controllers are doing is approved by the viewing figures. It is sanctioned by the television audience.

The buzzword now is 'event'. Event television is what you hope gets in the papers the next day. If you are unlucky, your event is *Gobble*, the turkey drama which became an event because it didn't happen at the right time and so it got in the papers for that reason. Soaps toddle along for months on end and then suddenly become an event when something sensational happens in them. *EastEnders* has so many events in it that one hasn't finished before the next begins: event drama with a small e. If you're lucky, a television event is the superb *Hillsborough*, the kind of excellence which will be used by the controllers to justify the health and wealth of television drama. *Hillsborough* might tempt anyone to say that television really does aspire to a ringing drama of social justice. But sadly, *Hillsborough* is one in a hundred: a drama which dealt with violent death so respectfully, in a way that maximized the horror through necessary restraint, as it were off-stage, in the Sophoclean way.

The opposite, in fact, of the same writer's enjoyable *Cracker*, where melodramatic violence is redeemed by clever psychology and human frailty. *Cracker* began as an event and ended, like so many television series, as a fixture. It would be an interesting line of discussion to question whether theatre too still seeks to be an event. And what recently might qualify.

When I had my first play put on at the Bush in the early 1980s, it was natural then for a successful play to be done on television, and a year and a half later it went out as a Play for Today. But now the single play on television is no more. Jonathan Harvey's *Beautiful Thing* has been made as a low-budget feature film. But why couldn't it have been seen on television as an Event? Or is it a story that *EastEnders* is already doing in a way executives think is more accessible? The certainty is that there is no easy home for playwrights on television. The sheer effort and rabbit it takes to convince someone that a good, serious idea will make a cracking three-part serial leaves you little energy for writing it.

But then the theatre is shrinking too and people are reading less novels. So where do we go from here?

David Eldridge was born and lives in Romford. His plays include *Serving it Up* (Bush, London), *A Week with Tony* (Finborough, London), the short plays *Cabbage for Tea, Tea, Tea* (University of Exeter/Platform 4) and *Dirty* (Theatre Royal Stratford East, 1996), and *Summer Begins* (Donmar Warehouse, 1997). His new play *Falling* opens at Hampstead in 1999.

Dusty Hughes was artistic director of the Bush Theatre, London, from 1976 to 1979. His stage plays include the award-winning *Commitments* (Bush), *Bad Language* (Hampstead Theatre), *Futurists* (National Theatre) and *A Slip of the Tongue* (Steppenwolf Theatre, Chicago, then Shaftesbury Theatre, London). His television work includes the final episodes of *Between the Lines* (BBC1), two episodes of *Call Red* (ITV), an episode of *Sharman* (ITV) and the opening episode of *The Broker's Man* (BBC1) in 1998.

PART THREE

Hold Your Nerve:
Notes for a Young Playwright

Phyllis Nagy

The contemporary theatre is decadent because it has lost the
feeling on the one hand for seriousness and on the other hand for
laughter; because it has broken away from gravity, from effects
that are immediate and painful – in a word, from Danger.
Antonin Artaud, c. 1938

Be brave. This is harder than it sounds. Because for one thing, we have
been led to believe that the act of putting pen to paper is bravery
enough. It is not. The decision to write a play is simply the start of a
complex moral process which never ends, not even with the production or publication of our plays.

And although most of us write alone, we do not write in isolation.
We write with the knowledge – sometimes comforting, at other times
terrifying – of the tens of thousands of plays which have preceded ours
and the many more to follow. What we write and how we write it are
informed directly by the social and political shifts of the societies we
inhabit, by the images and aural landscape of our popular culture. As
long as we draw breath, our writing evolves only by the process of
engagement with the 'other': other people, other cultures, other
political systems, other religious beliefs.

So we do not, must not, write in isolation. Because with isolation
comes insularity and narcissism, which in turn lead to a collapse of
bravery. Once that happens, the possibility for danger in our work is
replaced with cynicism. And once that happens, decadence sets in.
Bravery in playwriting starts with recognizing the necessity for the
dangerous.

Bravery is also difficult because cultural pundits constantly tell us what
our work is really concerned with. Apparently, the abiding preoccupation of plays and playwrights in the 1990s is the crisis of masculinity.
Men, we are told, have lost their identities in the home, in the

workplace – and by logical extension, in the theatre – and playwrights have begun to reclaim a male identity which was presumably lost without us noticing. The implication being that this was going on whilst women made stealthy but steady gains in the home, the workplace – and by logical extension, in the theatre. But this analysis seems, at least as far as the theatre is concerned, more like a slightly hysterical response to the gains of a very few women by the ever-robust theatrical disposition of a whole lot of men. It is interesting that because batches of plays in the 1990s have, on their surfaces, concerned themselves with the pursuits (primarily social or sexual) of young men, media commentary chooses to define the themes or preoccupations of these plays solely by means of their literal components.

The real subject of much serious drama written in this decade is not the crisis of masculinity – no more so than the crisis of feminism, say, might have been regarded by some as the preoccupying concern of late 1970s through mid 1980s drama. Rather, our concern, now as then, as always, is the collapse of our collective bravery, our daring and our imagination – regardless of individual narratives or what cultural commentators interpret as the literal concerns of this work. When Artaud spoke of theatrical danger and decadence in the 1930s, he may as well have been speaking to us from Birmingham in the 1990s, pre-Christian Athens or from any place where plays were written at any time in history we might care to choose.

The literal workings of the world and its minutiae have never been, and must never become, anything other than the tools we use to construct lateral work, which communicates metaphor. Without metaphor, art does not exist. And literalism is the enemy of metaphor. Literalism is attractive because it is immediately satisfying: we are presented with a set of events, behaviours or ideas which do not represent or suggest other related events, behaviours or ideas – but which instead seek to tell us nothing more or less about those events, behaviours or ideas than the fact that these things exist in our world. Because we already know these things to exist, we can remain comfortable in their presence. Reason tells us that it is only when we are comfortable with information that we can understand the information. And understanding something makes us feel smart. In this way, the flat-line of literalism is tremendously seductive. Who doesn't want to be understood? Who doesn't want to feel smart?

But somewhere along the line, we have forgotten that truly dangerous art never seeks to be merely understood. It seeks to communicate, with all the mystery and danger that word implies. The literal, though sometimes dangerous, is rarely mysterious, by definition. This is why we rely on and, indeed, implicitly trust serious journalism to report on the major events of our times: what the journalists tell us about ourselves and our political leaders may be unpleasant or even repellent, but we don't reject the information because it is both literally 'true' and lacks 'mystery'. We therefore comfortably accept, digest and understand the news. And crucially, the news is understood by us in the moment we take it in. We do not need to ponder over it in order to grasp its meaning on a literal level. This is what makes the experience essentially comfortable.

However, plays are not journalism. We do need to ponder over the meaning of good plays beyond the moment in which we watch them. This is the essence of resonance. Thus, plays can never be satisfying on the literal level of reportage. They are not merely the sum of their events. Being what it is, journalism (and therefore journalistic theatre criticism) necessarily seeks to remove the mystery from plays (and therefore their danger), as critics report on them as if they can be reduced to their literal, factual components for the benefit of any potential audience. And when it is impossible to attain either an instant understanding of plays or an instant sense of how to describe them for others, the natural tendency of commentary is to reject such work as being incoherent or incomprehensible.

But it is impossible to convey a sense of the lateral through the literal and so, with all the best intentions, journalistic criticism does not communicate to its audience any sense of the complexity of metaphor or emotion our plays might carry with them. This is how and why the question of what our plays are 'about' has come to be confused with what our 'themes' are. Plots, no matter how fractured or fragmented, can be conveyed literally and very nearly objectively. Of course, conveying plots and concluding that that's pretty much the sum total of what a play is 'about' is ever so much more satisfying than attempting to engage subjectively with a deeper, more fluid meaning of plays – with the *subtext* of meaning. Because bravery also involves engaging with the subjective, and therefore uncontrollable or unpredictable, elements of our work.

*

Engaging with the 'other' does not mean agreeing with it. In fact, true engagement comes only when we embrace and empathize with ideas, attitudes and systems of belief we disagree with or fear. Empathy is stimulated in equal measure by both fear and fearlessness of those traits we recognize in humanity but do not necessarily comprehend. Recognition is not enough. On its own, recognition merely simulates an empathetic response: recognition reminds us of the trait, but does not communicate the trait itself. Recognition with comprehension – engagement – involves what might be called the higher intellect and therefore, by necessity, true emotion as opposed to sentimentality. And it is a very brave playwright indeed who sees that there is no courage without fear, no fear without fearlessness.

But our fears as writers must not mirror the fears of the literal world, even as the pressure to deliver the literal 'goods' is at its most urgent. It is no use at all to write plays in which we simply affirm the usual, proper fear and horror of war, poverty, political unrest and social indifference. Again, this reduces the power of communication – of communion with an audience – to its basest, most literal arguments. Most importantly, the blind affirmation of thesis, the comfortable reiteration of what we already know to be fact, offers nothing but a vast hopelessness. Because developing just one side of an argument rejects the very duality which makes us humane; the blanket rejection of the 'other' encourages shallow and cynical thought. This may be attractive for sound-bite analysis, but it is the antithesis of provocative analysis. Provocation, because it stimulates thought, offers us a way forward. It puts us on the road to hope. Only metaphor offers hope. And metaphor is definitively lateral.

It is ironic that much of what is currently valued in contemporary playwriting as being politically or morally incisive is really just artful reportage from the front lines, as it were, of popular culture or politics. That this reportage lacks intellectual rigour or even curiosity should alarm us. But the celebration of this kind of playwriting sends us, and our audiences, an urgent and terrifying message: that it is absolutely fine, in fact preferable, to lack any intellectual curiosity, which is increasingly seen as the enemy of popular culture. Though, in fact, intellectual curiosity is popular culture's necessary partner – its life-support system, if you will.

Our failure to realize that a lack of intellectual curiosity leads to a lack of emotional empathy is the real tragedy of contemporary theatre.

We live in an age of feeling, the media tells us. Of getting 'back in touch' with our emotions. And this, in our work, translates into a return to 'subject-driven' (i.e. emotional) plays and a rejection of 'form-obsessed' (i.e. intellectual) plays. Even those who run our theatres, sometimes especially those who run our theatres, speak the most ridiculously and reductively on this topic. It is sheer nonsense. Emotion does not occur without the intellect; the intellect is stimulated only by strong emotion. It is a mistake to believe that there is such a thing as a theatre of 'feeling' as opposed to a theatre of 'thought'. One does not occur without the other, ever, in plays that resonate. But it can be difficult to distinguish between sentiment and sentimentality, between rigorous intellectual pursuit and intellectual sleight-of-hand.

Plays without form are meaningless. To suggest that it is possible, even preferable, to have plays in which content is more important than form is ridiculous. Any single word has content. But an exchange of dialogue has a form. If it does not, we grow bored. No matter how compelling the subject of a play, if the manner in which it is conveyed to us does not shape its content, we will forget that play the moment it ends. It is the way most stories are told, not the stories themselves, which creates emotional intensity. Those who fear form 'overwhelming' content in plays mistakenly overlook this.

Perhaps we can most easily recognize the way form shapes emotional response through television journalism. The same breaking story about an airline crash viewed from the perspectives of several networks illustrates the principle well. The plot of the crash is fixed. What changes is the particular emphasis placed on the details of the narrative by individual reports. Depending on the selection of detail, we may experience – and therefore respond emotionally to – the story in different ways: a panorama of scattered plane parts seeks to depersonalize the tragedy; interviews with survivors seek to highlight the retention rather than the loss of life; rows of body bags in fields or marshes seek to remind us of the shocking and sudden brutality of death; and so on. The way in which our emotions engage with a story while we watch it unfold – in other words, while that story is being communicated to us in the moment – depends entirely on how a writer chooses to relate its events.

The example of television journalism is also useful as it reminds us that what we see now carries more weight than what we hear. This is because, through television and film, the way we learn to receive and process information has changed. Before television and film were widely accessible, the word was our primary source of communication – spoken or written. Photographs, especially in the context of print journalism, engaged our imaginations rather than rendered them useless, because of the literal inertia of photographs. Only a single moment of a narrative is contained in a photograph – but it is nonetheless a narrative moment. We must imagine what happens in the time before and after that photograph is taken in order to complete or extend the narrative. In that way, photography, like good play-writing, invites active participation from its audience. The very moment the photographer chooses to show us in his picture necessarily dictates the narrative we will then attempt to construct around the image.

When we tell people about the plays or films we have seen, our language becomes almost entirely visual. But we translate the visual through the use of the word. Perhaps without realizing it, what we do when we talk about the experience of seeing plays is exactly what we must do in order to write them well. We do not relate narrative detail through dialogue, but rather through image structure, which is built not simply from a literal series of images, but from the collision of word and image. And though a single image tends to be more potent than a single word, they are interdependent for the purposes of creating metaphor. One without the other serves only to remind us of thoughts or feelings we already have. But separately, they do not create thought or feeling. Together, they do. And together, they define form.

It is only after a story is told, when we no longer actively participate in its telling, that we may begin to analyse our response to it. Excellent plays demand that audiences participate in the unfolding of their narratives by requiring them to simply watch and listen. These are not passive actions. Communication involves active parties. But the moment a play allows its audience to analyse its intentions while it is being performed, the audience becomes passive, and thus the experience of the play is passive. An audience ceases to participate in the unfolding of a play because analysis during the event itself prohibits communication – by nature a lateral, associative experience. When we can connect the dots while we watch a play, that play becomes nothing more than the literal sum of its parts.

However, the temptation to consciously connect the dots in our work is great for a number of reasons. In the first instance, when we discuss our plays with dramaturges they insist upon answers – but the questions they ask are almost always of a literal nature. Such as 'why' people behave in a certain manner in a certain play. What they fail to realize is that the behaviour of characters in the context of the event is the answer. Also, there is never a single satisfactory answer to a complex question. This is not to imply that we should not be able to rigorously discuss the motivations of behaviour in our work. If we can't, then our plays are incoherent. But if we are able to definitively answer questions about why our plays exist or what they mean, then our plays do not allow for active communication with an audience. But sometimes our plays are programmed because they can and do definitely answer such questions to the satisfaction of misguided dramaturgy.

It is also nearly impossible to overcome the preconceptions our audiences necessarily bring to the theatre about the way stories ought to be told. This is not, as condescending media and theatre practitioners alike would have us believe, because audiences are dumb. It is because television and film have radically altered the form in which we receive most stories. When we speak generally about the degenerating effect television and film have had on the theatre, we make the mistake of attributing the degeneration to their content – to the quality and quantity of the ideas they present us with. But it is the passivity and mental laziness their forms promote that cause trouble. If theatre is a truly active form of communication, then the passivity of any potential audience will kill us.

Finally, theatre criticism itself encourages and congratulates passivity because most theatre critics seem to believe that it is desirable to analyse a play while they watch it. That instead of taking an active responsibility for answering the questions plays raise, audiences should not have to 'work too hard'. If this is true, then there is nothing moral – and therefore spiritually, emotionally or intellectually illuminating – about the experience of watching a play. Some of the key components of morality (responsibility, activity, participation) are actually replaced with some of the key components of decadence (indifference, passivity, inertia).

The danger in our current theatrical climate is that instead of fighting the death-knell of passivity, we have adopted a self-congratulatory if-you-can't-beat-'em-join-'em attitude to our work as playwrights. We convince ourselves that by utilizing film and television techniques in our plays, by answering more questions than we raise, by doing nothing other than presenting a self-evident thesis to our audiences, we are actually communing with them. We second-guess the expectations of 'young' audiences and speak excitedly about the 'numbers' of people flocking back to the theatre. We assume they are 'coming back' because we have hit upon a new way to speak to them. What we have really done is to give them the same information they get from television and film – because we necessarily all tell the same stories over and over again – in exactly the same *form* these media already provide. If experimentation with form in art, in concert with content, enables us to challenge or explore our behaviour in order that we might move forward, then what is the possible use of celebrating or encouraging the blurring of formal distinction in the various artistic media?

This tendency towards a theatrical passivity also accounts for a proliferation of topical drama, which purport to be 'hard-hitting' or 'cutting-edge' examinations of life as it is. But that is all it is. Such work simply confirms what we already think we know to be truth. Consequently, such work is cynical and narcissistic because it plays on this knowledge and allows us to remain at a safe distance from the events portrayed. We are never provoked by safety. So from the safety of perspective, we confuse the topical with the radical. Most plays which deal with violent sexual practices, drug-taking and general nihilism, utilizing filmic or televisual techniques in an effort to engage their audiences, actually alienate them. And while they are certainly topical, they are almost never radical.

The suspicion, bordering on contempt, with which rigorous intellectual and ideological pursuit is regarded in the current theatrical climate has led to a laziness in the pursuit of our craft. The confusion of a static, episodic, essentially televisual structure with a pure theatrical structure fusing metaphor with narrative is evident in much of this decade's work. Plays which shift locale from Timbuktu to London may be episodic but not necessarily theatrical, whereas plays which keep their characters firmly rooted to a sofa may be deeply and thrillingly theatrical. But we learn to tell the difference only by maintaining a continual connection to plays other than our own.

We must read them, see them, talk about them. Constantly. And not only the plays of the past, but especially the plays of the present.

And we must not forget that popular culture is our greatest resource. We are led to believe that theatre – like opera – is a culture discrete unto itself, having little or no connection to other, more popular art forms like television or film, even though we increasingly try, however misguidedly, to ape the forms such media take in an effort to be as 'popular' as they are. But it is a mistake to equate popularity in the context of culture with numerousness. Rather, it is more useful to begin to equate popularity with commonality (as opposed to the commonplace), in the sense that popular culture is what we, all of us, truly hold in common as a singular point of reference. As a springboard from which we make our leaps into imagination. Popular culture is not just television, film or pop music. It is politics, sports, fashion, religion – in short, those things which shape and affect our opinions or emotions. And the manner in which these things present themselves to us is equally important. Culture, like plays, is never merely the sum of its content.

In an age where theatrical form is ambiguous, it can be very hard to hold one's nerve. Every other day, somebody else tells us that writing has either lost its primacy in the theatre, or that in fact such primacy never existed. That we writers are churlish when we seek to maintain the integrity of a single, abiding vision that yearns to communicate itself to willing audiences. Some have even gone as far as to suggest that in reality, texts are not 'authored' by writers, but are created by collaboration with other theatre practitioners. That the very notion of 'text' implies a stasis we must somehow overcome if theatre is to remain vital.

We must resist this kind of thinking with every fibre of our beings. Plays are *written*. They are usually written by a single person in possession of an idiosyncratic style and point of view. Collaboration is necessary in order that a play exists in three dimensions for an audience on a particular evening. Collaboration is necessary in the creation of theatre, but not in the creation of text. A single, intelligent, evocative and compelling point of view which is interpreted by collaboration creates theatrical excitement. When point of view is muddied or unfocused by the textual contributions of many people, such excitement is usually diluted and dulled.

131

Text is present in every piece of theatre, even in theatre without dialogue or in improvisational theatre. Because the moment one person performs a single action on a stage, the moment a person decides (and it *is* a decision, a *choice*) to speak a particular word, or to utter a particular sound, there is narrative placed within a specific context. And such narrative is authored whether or not we choose to acknowledge it. Like it or not, it is for this very reason that text, and therefore plays, have and always will have primacy in our theatre. Because without our texts, our collaborators have nothing to do.

While this is comforting, it is also terrifying. Because the ultimate responsibility for ensuring engagement with and vibrancy in our art rests firmly with us. If we do not safeguard the traditions and integrity of playwriting, if we allow our spirit and craft to decay, if we sanction a further erosion of form, then theatre really must die. Unless we gamble that in maintaining our nerve as writers (as opposed to thinking of ourselves as people who simply work in the theatre) we will preserve what is extraordinary in theatre, there is no reason to continue. It's as simple and exasperating as that. Like all good gamblers, we must understand that in order to hit the jackpot, we have to not only recognize but court loss as a necessary component to winning big. All gamblers intuitively know that losing and being right are two different things. And however reckless or irrational such a position might seem to be, it also manages to encompass the moral duality that all great art aspires to. So let's roll the dice one more time. We have everything to play for. Be brave.

Phyllis Nagy's plays include *Weldon Rising, Butterfly Kiss. Disappeared, The Strip* and *Never Land.*

APPENDIX

The Birmingham Theatre Conference

1990 Regional Accents

Michel Vinaver, Ann Jellicoe, Peter Terson, Stephen Lowe, Burt Caesar, Don Kinch, Segun Ojewuyi, Susan Todd, Noel Greig, Julie Wilkinson, Gwenda Hughes, Guillem Jordi Graells, John McGrath, Tony Clark, John Godber, Jane Thornton, Bill Morrison, Robert David MacDonald, Jude Kelly, Clare Venables, Jatinder Verma, Debbie Horsfield, Claire Luckham, Willy Russell, Alan Dossor, John Adams, Pat Trueman, Christopher Honer, Peter Cheeseman, Melanie Harris, David Farnsworth, Ian Brown

1991 State of Play

Paula Milne, Anthony Minghella, Alan Plater, Ian Brown, Winsome Pinnock, Clare McIntyre, Louise Page, Bryony Lavery, Alby James, David Holman, Christopher Hampton, Charlotte Keatley, Trevor Griffiths, Lloyd Trott, Polly Thomas, Tony Craze, Caroline Kay, Mel Kenyon, Charles Hart, Melanie Harris, Michael Imison, David Thacker, Michael Attenborough, Max Stafford-Clark, Richard Eyre

1992 Beyond Words

Cicely Berry, Hilary Westlake, Nancy Meckler, Arnold Wesker, Phyllida Lloyd, Jenny Topper, Harriet Walter, Kenny Ireland, Terry Johnson, Lev Dodin, Michael Stronin, Alison Steadman, Stephen Bill, Mike Leigh, Sheila Kelly, Geraldine Pilgrim, Denise Wong, Vayu Naidu, Roger Marsh, Vic Hoyland, Michael Coveney, Annabel Arden

1993 National Stages

Bill Alexander, John Fox, Chris Hannan, Dalia Ibelhauptaite, Christopher Kalomgera, Constantine Dzhabarov, Vitali Malakhov, Femi Osofisan, Michael Pearson, Ian Brown, Edward Thomas, Jorg Mihan,

Anatoli Smelyanski, Liudmila Razumovskaya, John McGrath, Rona Munro, Christina Reid, Yvonne Brewster, Jatinder Verma, Richard Gough, Thomas Kilroy

1994 All Passion Spent?

Michael Billington, John Bull, John Godber, Philip Hedley, Jules Wright, Andy de la Tour, Ron Rose, Jane Thornton, Bryony Lavery, Charlotte Keatley, Sharman Macdonald, Alma Cullen, Mary Cutler, Michael Eaton, Rob Richie, Neil Bartlett, Jackie Guy, Stephen Lowe, Annie Castledine, Liz Lockhead, Max Stafford-Clark, Sam Mendes

1995 Facing the Music

John Caird, Adam Pollock, Stephen Banfield, John Owen Edwards, Adrian Mitchell, Jude Alderson, Dave Rogers, Gwenda Hughes, Michael Coveney, Tom Sutcliffe, Alain Boublil, Kate Edgar, Andre Ptaszynski, Mark Steyn, Julian Grant, Nick Dear, Jonathan Dove, Meredith Oakes, Michelene Wandor, Graham Vick, Judith Weir, Jan Smaczny, Richard Stilgoe

1996 Reality Time

Derek Paget, Robert Smallwood, Ian McBride, Sita Williams, Rob Ritchie, Michael Eaton, Roger Graef, Patrick Swaffer, Oliver Goodenough, Paula Milne, Rona Munro, Martin Crimp, Ian Curteis, Howard Brenton, Michael Hastings, Terry Johnson, Peter Whelan, John Mortimer, Christopher Hampton, Sebastian Barry, Oliver Ford Davies, Maggie Steed, David Calder, Timothy West, Mark Lawson

1997 About Now

Peter Ansorge, Mark Ravenhill, William Gaminara, Kevin Elyot, Clare McIntyre, Rebecca Prichard, Winsome Pinnock, Doug Lucie, David Greig, Cheryl Martin, Andy de la Tour, Dusty Hughes, Catherine Johnson, David Eldridge, Phyllis Nagy, Stephen Poliakoff, Robin Arthur, Diane Samuels, April de Angelis, Timberlake Wertenbaker, Anne Devlin, Conor McPherson, Bill Morrison, Mike Bradwell, Stephen Daldry, Teresa Topolski, Nicholas Wright

1998 Better Red

Chris Rawlence, Glen Park, Richard Stourac, Libby Mason, Mala Hashmi, Richard Seyd, Noel Greig, Maya Chowdhry, Pam Brighton, Gilly Hanna, Winsome Pinnock, Howard Brenton, Annie Castledine, Patrick Wright, Dorothy Hobson, Michael Kustow, Tariq Ali, John McGrath, Jenny Sealey, Roland Muldoon, Alison Andrews, Maggie Ford, Kully Thiarai, Paul Heritage, Anthony Sargent

1999 Losing the Plot?

Janelle Reinelt, Dan Rebellato, Stephen Jeffreys, Phyllis Nagy, April de Angelis, David Eldridge, Shelagh Stephenson, Mark Ravenhill, Sarah Woods, Annabel Arden, Michael Pearson, James Yarker, David Lodge, Malcolm Bradbury, Andrew Davies, Andrea Earl, Tilly Black, Lucy Gough, Mary Cutler, Michael Eaton, Paula Milne, Tony Marchant, Vayu Naidu, Charlotte Keatley, Jon Oram, Rosy Fordham